RUNNING BEF

RUNNING BEFORE THE WIND

Poems about the Sea

Edited by Joy Howard

GREY HEN

First published in 2013 by Grey Hen Press
PO Box 450
Keighley
West Yorkshire
BD22 9WS
www.greyhenpress.com

ISBN 978-0-9552952-9-4

Collection Copyright © Joy Howard 2013

Copyright in each poem remains with the authors

Printed by: Flexpress, Birstall, Leicester. LE4 3BY

For all voyagers. May you come safely home.

for whatever we lose (like a you or a me),
it's always our self we find in the sea.

e e cummings

Preface

'It is ungenerous, not to be trusted for a moment, without character or will of its own, reflecting the sky, following the moon, and driven by the wind.'*

So why are we drawn to, and love as well as fear the sea? The poems in this book help us to get to grips with some of these often conflicting emotions.

There are many evocative and powerfully recognisable descriptions to be found, but at heart these are inevitably personal responses. For we each have to make our own accommodation with the unbiddable two-thirds of our planet, whose influence is potent, but whose immensity is almost unimaginable.

Joy Howard

* Anne Treneer 'The Sea in English Literature'

Contents

the salt-lashed voyage

a great watery breath

where land forgets to be land

a bite of the salted air

to have seen these things

an absolute universe

that wet fist

the wide horizon

the constant taste of salt

the tide which will come

claiming the ocean

something in the blood

the oldest dream

the salt-lashed voyage

Seafarer

longe sceolde / hreran mid hondum / hrimcealde sae
(from the Anglo-Saxon poem *The Wanderer*)*

I'm the one in the lifeboat
After the ship went down:
O never pity me for
The salt-lashed voyage home.

I'm the one undrowned
(Though I have come
Sorrowing seas across –
And the rest gone).

Gerda Mayer

* For a long time / he must move with his hands / the ice-cold sea.

a great watery breath

At First Sight

Your breath is almost lost.
Your eyes can't hold it all.

It's huger than huge.
Out of the sky mist this flat
marvel stretches in every
direction, making a sad sound.

It slides its overlapping
scales nearer. White claws
snatch, retreat, gouge channels,
devour the land you stand on.

Unsleeping, it roars, howls,
hisses, froths, crashes and creeps.
Night and day you listen.
Its susurration is ceaseless.

It drinks rain, whirls up wind,
sings storms with its crashing
glass walls and crushed stones,
swallows ships, vomits detritus.

Its tang is of salt and weed
as it rises and falls.
Coloured deeper than its
mother sky, ever-changing.

Full of green rot and dark
shapes, its silver surface
glitters and glistens, reflects
the sun and moon in spangles.

Birds swoop down to peck
its belly full of fish.
Translucent paperweight eyes
are jellyfish along its edges.

It fills all the spaces in your
knowledge and imagination.

Jenny Morris

from **Different Tides**

The sea absorbs us with mountainous unconcern
getting on with its own business pulling and pushing
smelling of salt and wildness even when there is no-one about to smell it
roaring and growling, dragging up shingle or bodies
or far away from land rolling like an enormous animal round the world,
                                                    turning in
and back on itself, coiling and recoiling, swallowing every shade of blue
                                                    and green
and taking them down into lightlessness

Christine Webb

The Straight Lines of Sea Areas

This is the shape of the sea in Malin:
Northerly backing westerly; good.
Herring catches down, Mallaig ailing
Cod endangered, glass falling.

This is the taste of the sea in Hebrides:
Herring-gulls – eggs a salt-fish-ness,
Young skua meat smoking in strips,
Crofts hooded with rain; occasionally poor.

This is the feel of the sea in Rockall:
Kelp slippyness, moon slivers rough
Or very rough, high racks of stormcloud,
Heavy swell all the way to Maine.

This is the sound of the sea in Bailey:
A screaming of white horses,
Teeth veering Force Eight; severe.
While, on sea bottom, boulders grind.

This is the smell of the sea in Faeroes:
Guano, boat diesel and Famous Grouse,
A tang of icebergs calving away North,
The lonely scent of coconuts on the Jetstream.

Char March

What the Sea Is

A sheet of crinkled foil; silver luminescence
on a diver on the quay; black shine
on the shed skin of his suit; high tide
and neap; the flood and dove; unlit chamber
for the fish we never see; Old English,
North, the Dead and Caspian; it's Galilee
and drawn by the moon; depths untapped;
blue end of a telescope and on that map
where dragons be; it's grey mist to our east;
closed inside a shell and free to spread
its silk around the globe. It's between
the devil and .... lost and found at,
fished from and marooned; over it to Skye
and all the way to Ireland, Atlantis
and America. It's submerged trees
and galleons; whale song and the path
to Holy Island; never more in England
than seventy miles away; land's memory;
wing lift of a tern on his god speed
journey; cold salt blanket when you're three
at Blackpool; wave that makes you gasp
and flops you over; it's your empty hand
that just held water; it's a writer
telling stories in the sand no one can read.

Jo Haslam

North Atlantic, in a Storm

The word waves is too friendly for this sea,
bringing to mind a disembodied royal hand
acknowledging the crowd,
or the corrugated playground of a beach.
Adding *thirty foot* is not enough.

The word *sea* is too safe,
suggesting the Med or Red or the Dead,
or even the silent Sargasso.

I try *the ocean, the main, the deep, the high,
the trackless watery waste*
but these words are man-made, human sized.

This is no place for people,
or their regulated, so precise vocabulary –
what words are equal to the task
of bringing this ferocity to the page?
I dip my toe in Thunderous,
I paddle among Mountainous.
I splash about in Awesome.

Drowning in adjectives, I give up –
describe myself instead: ashamed and small,
as if I had just been introduced to God,
and couldn't think what to say.

Ann Alexander

Night Watch

In deepest night the ocean's wide expanse
Looks up to see a million points of light.
You stare into the sky until the dance
Of stars puts all terrestrial thoughts to flight.
Down here, the inky darkness blindfolds you,
The far horizon vanished into black;
No starshine shows that sea and sky are two –
Unseen the following waves pick up your track.

Narrow your thoughts into the commonplace;
Down the companion ladder, where the glow
Of crimson nightlight shows a human face –
Horror retreats, but lies in wait below.

Below the friendly cabin where you sit
Lies the deep ocean, dark and infinite.

Hermione Sandall

Sea Shades

Today the sun is a pale round window
in a thundercloud wall. Waves roar
and crash drowning out gull screams.
The pull of the moon rules these
flint-coloured, foam-mouthed
hunting beasts whose relentless surge
in the whirl of tides makes cliffs crumble,
walls shatter, small craft splinter.
Shores hide haunted hamlets lost
to the sea, flooded by invading water.
The coast sinks, bells toll in the deep.

In jade and sapphire, the outer sea
carries strange cargoes: sailors' shrouds,
poison bottles, driftwood, sharks' teeth.
In marble and jet, shuddering, it swallows
children, fish shoals, ships and oil slicks.
With salt on its lips, it spits out secrets:
amber, bones, keys and samphire
among bleached blooms of spindrift
on the shingle. At the far edge
the sea jaws crunch. Now
it devours the sun.

Jenny Morris

The Peaceful Sea

The great earth is doing what she does.
What she has always done at half an inch
a year. Shifting, easing her ischium,
hefting shoulders and scraping vertebrae
each one against the next. She's coughing up
her silicates to crust along the edges
of her plates. She's sucking in sea-bed
and slapping ocean across the basin
between her continents, only to yawn
and settle back content. Don't ask
about the dead, the lost, the unidentified.
She needs no numbers. She wants no names.

Anne Stewart

Sea View

We always want it don't we, with its promise
of infinity; the way it opens out
to that heart stopping colour
the Greeks had no word for. This one
in the bay's curve, a lovely half moon
you'd think you could step into, its water
warm against your skin. In truth
it's nothing like; the path is long and overgrown;
at every bend you think you're there
but no; and when you come to it at last
the water's leaden grey and lapping cold
against the shingle. The dark has come
without your noticing and the path
is still falling and falling away.

Jo Haslam

15

The Sea at Night

It crouches, heavy with threat,
so dark you hardly see the grey line
where earth meets sea meets sky.
Like some animal,
the sea always keeps one eye open.

The terrifying weight of water
leaning to the moon's pull
covers the earth, brooking no argument,
hearing no plea as it grinds out
its gravelly song.

I stand on the edge, uncertain underfoot,
salty fingers strip the shingle
from beneath my feet, tipping me back.
The black sea approaches,
retreats, beckons, repels.

When I am dead
lay me in the cold earth, dearest,
a thorn at my head, rock at my feet.
I am for dry land.

Ann Alexander

Take to the Sea

Sit this one out on the westermost promontory.
Track ghost hulks with black rigging
knitted plumb to the skyline. Schedule
the outward for a lifting tide.
Round trip perhaps.
                    Leave Sunday at dawn:
a partial eclipse augurs. Tap the mercury.
Chart trade winds. Some guesswork.
A north-easterly would be a godsend. Rely
on your eighth sense. Observe estuary
mudlarks for clues.
                    Give the harbourmaster
your route-map, in case. Some aren't seen
for decades.

A single knapsack with pouches, chrome yellow
oilskins, a dog-eared polaroid from when you
met, blanched almonds for basecamp soirées.

A fall of snowgeese startles you back to Lir's
children, the icy struggle. Slide-show memories:
helter-skelter seafront music, garlands
of coloured bulbs, postcards from your children:
imprints you'll need if it gets to that.
                    Enough
to see you through twisters, squalls. Allow yourself
a parting phonecall, holler over static on the seabed
cable, make sure you're heard across the Forties.

Anne-Marie Fyfe

The Weather in the Sea is Dying

and weather once drove the tides
up over the land in a great watery breath.

Slock tilt rock – planar waves still tip
randomely over the silt where the dead weather lies

long after the land has slid like a plate
off its draining board – though the sea

keeps for itself just a small glass of weather
to diddle the seaweed fronds

in a last lazy riff while bones build almost
to the roof of the water

and shells are still growing
sly as dead finger nails.

Isn't it peaceful?
Think of it now if you can.

No creature then
to think the unthinkable calm.

Kate Foley

The Dream is the Ocean

The ocean calls the dolphin
      The dolphin calls the wave
The wave calls the sun
      The sun calls the coral
The coral calls the colour
      The colour calls the fire
The fire calls the moment
      The moment calls the light
The light calls the shine
      The shine calls the spray
The spray calls the deep
      The deep calls the dolphin
The dolphin calls the dream
      The dream is the ocean

Katherine Gallagher

where land forgets to be land

Norfolk Coast

This is where land
forgets to be land,

sea loses track
of being the sea,

sky lets go
of horizon after horizon.

Here's a beach
so far from its harbour

sky-blue boats
are moored a mile inland

and you have to take a train
to reach
the turn-of-the-tide.

This is where water
keeps unmaking its mind –

fresh, salt? –

flitting from creek to pool,
from estuary loop to ebbing reach,

and where the pinewoods
are a law unto themselves,

spurning inundations,
roots holding the soil in thrall,

lifting sky and cloud so high
they have nowhere else to go but dusk...

Penelope Shuttle

Chesil Beach

Love is water, our shared history, stone;
each encounter alters us a little.

*

These limestone rocks
are records of the sea's wide journeys.
Rollers have pummelled them with glassy tons,
        or played tame, froth kissing their skins;
have brought them the world's particles,
        carried some away.

Stones get a taste of life like this;
and water daily meets its limitations.

Exchange,
        exchange;
                both are changed by it.

*

Each of us is water,
each is stone;
how difficult
to map those elements
in one another, truly.

*

A few mayfly decades can't comprehend
how long this shoreline has been trading
with the sea, in an alliance of opposites.

What constellation of improbabilities
has placed a trilobite or scrap of fern
inside some of these stoic rocks

as water, rhetorical and moody,
has lavished inexhaustible experience
in wearing stones into these shapes, these?

*

*Now
and again
let's hold one another to the light
as if each were the one stone in the world,
as if there's no end to illumination.*

*

Collectors, beady with desire,
raise their fossil hammers,
smash randomly
the smooth grey bellies of the stones
and, seeing mainly absence,

leave almost all,
inner worlds exposed
for the first time ever;
brown, grey, ochre chronicles
enlightening no one.

Who cares? Not stones.
As water sluices
round their splintered hearts,
with unimaginable slowness
they are becoming sand.

Carole Satyamurti

Current

A hundred yards along the beach, bent
on a cross-legged stool –
that's him alright, that's his flapped hat
and dark waxed jacket, his way
of sitting, shoulders stooped, back braced to the wind

watching the sea at the end of his line,
the sea he reels in, the immensity of it,
only the propped rod
breaking the level, leaning towards the waves
that roll in along this shore
at a distinctive, particular diagonal,
foaming sideways, a sly suck and flow

if you're swimming; you can be a hundred yards
down the coast without knowing it,
glancing up and seeing that the same
is not the same at all – not quite
the amount of sand, the little cliffs
higher, brambles and sea kale now at their foot
and someone who might have been
for a moment your father fishing.

Caroline Price

North Sea, 1940

Barbed wire was one thing:
Torn gym-slips testified
To its intricate weave. As it rolled
Along the cliff-top, sharp and shining,
It might have slowed him down.

The sea was another thing entirely.
Not dainty like the Channel, it foamed
Four hundred miles to the other side to
Schleswig-Holstein (we knew). With Hitler
Probably, impatient on the shore.

Was it the sea that stopped him?

It wasn't our guns. While searchlights
Fingered the dark, a whole street vanished.

The sea spoke, all night long,
Hushing against the shore.
The beach was *Out of bounds*. The cliffs
Out of bounds. Who cared? But the sea
Told tales to my mother through
My shoes, with their tide-line of salt.

The sea was grey-green
Like a German uniform; was
Chill, familiar, seductive;
More real than Hitler.

Daily the sea swallowed the horizon, daily
It savaged our bit of England. Unlike Hitler
It always knew when to stop.

R V Bailey

Sea Wall, Overy Staithe

Running   I become
the bank's long legs
and bendy knees
Sometimes I outwit time
a quickening into the moment
knowing every step
will take me somewhere
                      different

Travellers with tripods
picnics   rucksacks   guns
worm-diggers
the cyclists and the day-trippers
have met my several selves –
patterns of early footprints on the dry sea-wall
loosing energy into the dunes
where space opens

Vermuyden's men
with weather-beaten faces
first walled up the sea
and now again
a team
         strip back to bones
the mallows   clover   chamomile
The driver, high on caterpillar tracks,
slaps and spreads grey clay emulsion

I am the length and breadth
of what's unchanged
am lapwing (disappearing)
butterflies in spiral
an acrobat (my shadow)
a natterjack (my song)
a windslam across the saltings
beneath enormous skies

People have gone
Trees that bore the dog rose
and the tiny self-sown apples
gone
Still   I run
look backwards and look forwards

I allow this running
to carry me beyond

Sally Festing

Erosion

On the west coast beach at low tide
we find shells dyed by seaweed
to the green of the marram grass.
Video cameras whirr and bleep, while
fighter planes blast through the air.
Seagulls watch from their distances.

We are too tired to take it in, too
dispirited, worn down like the shells
and the rocks until we too are like
the sand slipping through our fingers,
being blown about by the wind.

We need to be held by the marram grass,
by the blue sea, the small isles in the distance,
the tide going out on a great sad sigh.

Rosemary McLeish

St. Andrews Harbour

The tide goes up and down against these walls
whose stones, unmortared, have withstood the years
of constant washing. Water rises, falls

with measured regularity, giving the piers
a shifting look. The tangled veil, now dried,
now soaked, of bladderwrack appears

and disappears according to the tide.
Herring-bone sand reveals its presence, then
submerges. Here, where land and sea collide,

one could fall off the edge. The elements
feel stronger here: air, water, earth and fire
distilled by wind as salt and oxygen.

History lurks, buried in sand and mire,
drowned sailors, rib-cage ships, dismembered dreams,
now lost in sea and sand, a world entire
where all is clear but nothing what it seems.

Lyn Moir

Shore to Ship

How difficult to gauge the passing time
on summer sands, clamour of gulls and boys,
a daze of sea, flat as tin, disinclines
any further thought: sun and warmth decoys.

The intermittent sweep of light on rocks
is barely visible in high noon sun:
a chill that will occasionally mock
returns to heat before the day is done.

The crust of salt from sea to land gives lie
to true intent, slyly begins its mark
as fluff of frost: yet sudden shift of sky,
a clatter of birds in the sullen dark

will leave no time to toll the change of watch
between the dogwatch and the deathwatch.

Ruth O'Callaghan

Sceilig Mhicíl

From turbulent Atlantic
a Cathedral rises
near perpendicular
jagged green-streaked black
possessed by wings and wails
of puffin, razorbill, kittiwake.

On the rockface
anchorite monks
hacked and hewed
sandstone and shale
six hundred steps
each chiselled chip a prayer.

Sea mist, salt incense
swirls from the summit
reveals two drystone
boat-shaped oratories
six beehive cells
a surprise of fertile green.

'Out, far out of this time
and this world',*
this shrine of praise and penitence,
place of pilgrimage,
survivor of Viking plunder,
gale whiplash, rainslant,
holds fast.

Bernie Kenny

* George Bernard Shaw

Alnmouth

Something unassuagable about an estuary.
Black ooze, oily,

Clinging. Dragging east,
Miles of cloud rubble.

Acres of sea-purslane.
Redshank, dunlin,

Camouflaged. Dissemblance.
Chains of footprints

Snaking through mud. Loops
Of old rope. A curlew

Letting go its rinsed notes.
Abandonment.

And, slowly filling with water,
A boat

Rotten beyond rescue, its anchor-chain
Stiff; paint, lichen,

Flaking from its timbers, revealing
Strong, clear lines. What matters

Is sunk, uncovered
And sunk. On the far bank, a train,

A straight line on the heugh,
Hauling its troubles south.

And between them, the river
Slipping from green fields, Scots pines, gables –

Pink, blue, terracotta –
From the gull-squabble,

Towards something sparer:

Wormcasts.
Ripples.

On the far side of the water,

Walls, roofless.
Gleaming bent grass.

Its surface wind-hatched, stippled with light,
The river

Is letting go
At the end of its life, an old man

Catching sight of what matters –
That muffled roar,

The stern white line of the breakers.

Katrina Porteous

Blakeney

Land is king here. The sea struggles
to keep its waterways between marsh and field.
In the harbour at low tide water dribbles
over sandbars and in the shallows gulls stand
on their doubles. The path to the coast is bone dry.
I love the miles of reeds straight as seabird legs.
They flame to orange where they've found moisture.
Skyblue pools succeed among grasses,
among glasswort clumps thronged by warblers.
And what is it I want – that pale strip
pulling me like a magnet, the unhookable sea
with ever-shifting glitter, the chance of slipping
from everyday clutter, wading in, undoing
flesh and letting the self loose in everness?

Myra Schneider

Charting the Tides

Sea thrashes the slump-backed Cobb that rounds
into the surf at Lyme, wearing away – over centuries –
its hard stone strength. We try to regulate our beaches
with flags and notices; to predict, calculate, tabulate
the tides, (high and low) and times of sunrise and sunset;
print figures in booklets (Dorset pink, a pound a throw –
No liability for exceptional weather conditions.).

Life tides, uncharted, swirl and trick us, some rising on a wave
of pills and pacemakers, washing over the old high-water mark
of three score year and ten – some falling, prematurely scuppered.

The beach, where tides gather and turn, has evolved
into a memorial garden, blackened by tar, encrusted
with metal junk from lost cargo and ships that have died;
two red flags, lifeless and torn by unfamiliar storms;
scraps of tiny sea creatures trapped in fossil spirals;
late features of cliff, crashed and ground to grit; shells
empty of life, broken and crunched into fragments;

We strengthen our sea walls with shingle, peg the hill with rods,
buy time – while waves falter, dissolving to a quieter rhythm,
foam absorbed into sand, footprints smoothed out by the sea.

June Hall

Slapton Sands

Back to the beginning, or so it seems
on Slapton Sands in the evening,
before night drops like a damp cloak
over distant hills, and shingled paths.

Walking along the beach, the hypnotic rhythms
of waves becoming part of myself, the indentations
of raindrops on water create small patterns,
and are gathered into the continuing rhythm;

the light diminishes, and trees on the headland
are not trees, but black smudges. This morning there
was an exultation of light, splinters of sun on water
and long sandbar shadows.

There is still enough light to see fronds of seaweed
patterning the shoreline, the small, empty crab shells
have a beauty like the stars,

a continuing beauty, like the book of hours.

Doris Corti

Making a Landscape

No sloping shore, no gradual trailing waves:
the sand stops, sliced sharply, the way peat is cut,
and here's the sea, lapping up to it, deep,
like a river in spate, a curdle of waves
rubbing the baulked edge of sand. But sea
can't be contained like this, sea has dug channels,
carved out its own particular curves, sculpting
slopes and ridges; and the channels
edge their way inland where sand turns to mud,
grown over with grass and purslane,
with thick-leaved plants that can survive salt-water
when the sea at high tide rushes in from the bay
fast as a galloping horse, leaps the wall of sand,
swamps channels, covers grasses,
swills driftwood almost to the road;
and submerges completely the place
where the sand, before it falls away so steeply,
is studded with shells, pinks and whites,
and between them the fine markings
which are the prints of seabirds' feet,
making an intricate landscape, almost a shoreline.

Elizabeth Burns

a bite of the salted air

Package Holiday

The dotted line, the furthest, is the rim of ocean
studded with tabs that might be ships.
press here to release the sky without tearing.

A second less distant horizon, look, leaks colour –
a stub of moving red, two greens.
Snip at this line to separate sea from sand.

Focus more closely until you observe the carton
of plastic and steel in which you are boxed
safe under blotted glass, flatpack shadow

staring at blanched explosions of paper birds
and the poorly laundered ocean edged
with yellowing lace. Should blades of sun slip through,

then risk a bite of the salted air: venture
seaward from shelter, flurrying and pausing,
one eye cocked like a flounder's for nets of rain.

M R Peacocke

At the Seaside

deep inland or far out at sea
there's no possibility of choice

there you are
there you stay

on the margins
you could go either way

turn your back on changeable water
for the sureness of mountains

or abandon the staid hills
for the buoyant variety of waves

here you straddle the edges
one foot in sand one in foam

delighted not to choose
under this wide waiting sky

Gina Shaw

With Seagull Cries

With seagull cries
Three diminutive girls
Tease the sea,
Thumb to nose.

One makes finger horns,
Charges her matador;
The curled cloak turns,
She shrieks back to the shore.

Far out, a rock
Becomes a Venetian glassblower;
Green, then transparent,
Hangs a trembling amphora;

And where the sea's grey blues
Pile up and congeal,
The sky's whirlpool
Draws up a white sail.

Hermione Sandall

Telescope

They line it up for me
and I am in a kittiwake's nest
on Kettleness Nab with skinny chicks
and a screaming mother who squashes me
with her warm breast. One jerk
and I've lost her. I'm flying now
past a lone fishing-boat,
lobster nets on a slipway
to a sandy beach where a man
who could be my uncle Frank
rows a broken dinghy.
On, on it goes until I reach
two figures on a rock. My eyes
can't focus. I think I see two
but they collide and separate
and merge again almost as though
they can't make up their minds.
Only the barnacles are clear
and the green bottle on the rock.
Then with a clunk the shutter drops
and there is only the pier
and the painted mine and a queue
of children who will see something different.

Carole Bromley

Written on the Beach, September

A nip in the sunny air,
but down on Castle Beach at 9 am
the sun's warm as breakfast toast,
the pale blue sea calm as a woodland pool,
sky a degree brighter,
just a brow of light grey cloud
over to the east.
The sun gets stronger by the minute.
The waves along the shoreline
can hardly be bothered to turn and slide back under.

A crabber drifts along on the calm water,
the crab-master hefting his baskets over the side.
With every minute the sea grows bluer,
the sky goes back into full summer mode,
glittering air of the still small morning.
Note, this is not the 'unique luminosity' of Los Angeles,
but of West Cornwall.

The crabber wheels round,
heads for another batch of marker buoys,
the lawn-mower drone of his engine
puttering across the bay.
There's a brief noisy routine turmoil
of herring gulls,
the silent regard of a band of oyster-catchers
(usually so prime-minister's question-time noisy)
and the blue hot September morning shines
like one of those clean-as-a-pin shells along the wet tide-line.

As I exit the beach,
a gust of cliff-swallows happens overhead,
little white bellies, scissor wings,
darting and volplaning,
higher and faster than the gulls,
a late-summer bravado of swallows,
show-offs, and why not?

Penelope Shuttle

45

Going West

A long distance from anywhere
you might remember. The last trees
were a while back. The hedges
sit tight, leaning inland. The air starts
to stick to your tongue and the map
reaches a final name.

There isn't very much to do, although
if you don't park with your back to the sea
you can glimpse Scotland when the cloud lifts,
so someone's troubled to work
on the notice until it advises

Please d i e carefully. Jack's Surf Bar
is where they discuss the perfect
wave. There was a perfect wave
once, and at Jack's
it goes on rolling, Pacific Blue,
crested and glassy, chariot of heroes.

Bingo was last Thursday. There is the Ship
and the Grapes. Before long, the surly sea
that is fed dropped chips and ice cream
will prowl and starve, the Leisure Centre have
more leisure that it can afford

and if you crunch out over the shingle
you can tell that the earth is flat.
Away down the coast, white masts
are fulling the salty air.
A solitary cormorant
tautens his line of flight

unerring over the keen waterchop,
fastening southerly to northerly,
one hard cusp of distance to another.
Two dogs with experienced grey muzzles
are laughing over something.

This is the place for men
and miniature men, for talk
of tides catches records goals. The women
sit. Older sitters have good big teeth,
and heads grown white like the blackheaded gulls
resigned to August.

(You don't expect a lad like the one down there,
the blue puffajacket, to be sitting alone,
his head bowed so low you might wonder,
but no it's all right, clamped
to his ear there's a mobile phone.)

This is a place to practice
the fine skills of waiting,
for a call, an encounter, a tug
on the line, for better luck: where almost
any pebble could turn out,
given an eye to discern it,

a wrist to flick it one step further
than the edge of the known ledged
brown world, to be a champion skipper,
could abandon once and for all the kingdom
of tearooms and a ragwort sun.

M R Peacocke

Desirable Residence

What do you *do* in a beach hut?
you cannot sleep in one
though the shush of the waves
would lull you in your eyeless cabin,
the cursing gulls awaken you.

You can only be English and sit,
out of the blast, cradling a mug,
or in the shade, mopping a brow
with a knotted linen handkerchief
while the children build

their impossible castles,
a helter-skelter for a ping-pong ball,
a tunnel under a splintered groyne,
and bent old men with sticks
and panting, rickety dogs,

wheeze a moment
against the verandah of Ma's Bar,
Misty, Katmandu, thinking
What do you *do* in a beach hut?
I mean what do you *do*?

You could have shuttered sex,
do dark, unmentionable things
with candy floss, a child's pail,
a little packet of flags
shake sand from boards

till it sways like the *Mary Lou*
jolts free of its locks,
hiccups across the prom
sheds skins of salt-bleached paint
across the shocked shingle

scatters corporation chairs,
tartan rugs, wind-breaks
crabbing nets and bladderwrack
and shudders rocking ten miles out
amid the cries of kittiwakes.

Carole Bromley

Davy, 7, Runs Away to Sea

The beach is anonymous, far from the damage people do.
Only the tide to listen and pay homage to, and follow it to Wherever,
far on the other side. Have faith, he tells himself. She – the honest

and loving sea – She'll provide what's needed. Enfoldment, a song
to soothe a troubled child, a fish or two. Get used to sand between the
toes,
avoiding jellyfish, and there you are – safe and free and home and dry.

And there were omens. A tender breeze, a bright cold sun. They cooled
his bruised and broken skin and dried his eyes, calmed his frantic mind.
Seagulls in the white clouds wheeled away, calling 'Come.' 'Come.'

Anne Stewart

Day Trip

Two women, seventies, hold hands
on the edge of Essex,
hair in strong nets,
shrieked laughter echoing gulls
as shingle sucks from under feet
easing in brine.

There must be an unspoken point
when the sea feels like
their future. No longer paddling,
ankles submerge in lace,
in satin ripple.
Dress hems darken.

They do not risk their balance
for the shimmering of ships
at the horizon's sweep
as, thigh deep, they inch on
fingers splayed, wrists bent,
learning to walk again.

Carole Satyamurti

Ebb Tide

Past 6 a.m. the waves retreat,
sky embellishes like stained glass. On the shore-line
gulls create calligraphy, our feet print patters.

Sapphire and opal the sea
as we turn from it, hear the day's sounds
buzz into our solitude. The drone of a car,
a child's urgent cry, dog yapping over a fence.

Leaning together under the sea-wall,
each a prop for the other, we shake sand
from our shoes.

Walking home our movements synchronise,
shoulders together, a timing of steps,
touching of hands eloquence enough, quiet rejoicing.

Climbing the hill to the house
the garden greets us, tumble of roses, lavender,
high hawthorn. Honeysuckle a trailblazer
we inhale its perfume, speak of breakfast.

Doris Corti

Floating

I unpin myself from the shore
swim out into sharp waves
toes still able to touch down on sand
but treading water, my arms

stroking the back of the sea
before I lie down into
the cold hand under my head,
sunshine bleeding umber

on the inside of my eyelids,
salt water – clear, green, fresh –
washing out weariness
in a rhythm of gentle breaths

breathing me onwards, incessant.
No wonder water is spiritual,
laces the foreheads of babies.
Cruciform, I am released into

the sky, fingers spread wide
as I float out on my back
and the white clouds scud over
and everything feels possible again.

Susanna Harding

Reprise

We learn again
the weave and pattern
of the pebbled shore

the early morning hush
amongst the lobster creels
and empty sheds

red hot pokers
bright as noon
splicing the marram grass

the beach at night,
rocks black
against a moon-lit sky

old summer clothes
slipped on once more
in a half-forgotten song.

Eleanor Livingstone

Whitley Bay

The sun's big moment. Balanced on top of the sea
His shining carpet unrolls. The intent rat,
Scavenging the cliffs, doesn't notice. The sea
Stretches itself; tries a little roar;
Settles down again.

Tides high. Dash in, dash out.
Goosepimpled regulars saltily
Gratefully dash back to breakfast.

Warm enough, in the sun, with your back to the promenade wall.
Crossword, knitting, sunglasses, flask;
Snooze here till lunchtime. Soft sand
Lets everything fall into place.

Gran's with the chapel trip.
She'll not come next year. It's nippy
Watching the canny bairns,
Watching the sea spread itself
All the way to Tynemouth.

And the bairns can't wait –
Fish and chips and candy floss,
A go on the big wheel,
Hours and hours and hours
On the sands.

The sea's sure of itself,
Knows its own highs and lows,
Comes every day, all year;
Has serious designs on the cliffs.

Under her *kiss me quick* hat, he does.
He makes a deep impression,
On her, on the beach. Sea
Sighs, turns over, sighs again. Sand
Lets it all wash over her.

Tide's right out now. Rocks, ribs,
Ridges: joined up lacy calligraphy
No one can read.

Sun and sea stir themselves.
Where's the wind come from?
When did the light go
From Bandstand, Esplanade, the Lower Prom?

The lovers have caught the sun. Behind the wind-break
Gran says she's caught cold. The bairns
Have caught it from the Da, for waking him up.

The coach drivers fold their *Mirrors*. On the sands,
Toffee papers, orange peel, crusts,
The forgotten watch.

R V Bailey

to have seen these things

Shoreline South West

Back where I'm from, the sea is hours away
and dead when you get there,
strangled by a thick rubber corset
of guesthouses run by hate-filled harridans.
Then the girdle of screaming switchbacks,
and finally the concrete death-band:
the promenade to keep the pebbles in order.

No one then told me about this joyous
limb of land kicking care-free out
into the dancing ocean.

I did not know then about fields that stopped
startled at the edge of air. About bracken
and brambles slithering madly down stony slopes
to the shore. I had not seen dock seedheads
burning rust against summer-white grass.

Nor hidden streams tickling the undersides
of meadowsweet and bedstraw.
Or ocean winds planing
the green slopes clean. I knew nothing
about seas that smashed, laughing,
and seals that watched.

It is worth growing older to have seen
these things.

Pat Simmons

Letter from Birsay

Because you've never stood on this beach,
never breathed in this sea, I'll describe the sheet
after sheet of rock compressed into tilted layers,
the stones, bleached orange and ice blue,
lying in heaps and straggles, the ribboning sand,
the causeway leading to the island's green mound.

Because you will not visit this shore, because
you wouldn't see what I do if you did, I want you
to know how the smell of lime weed and salt
jumps me to a beach where water seeped into
our soft castles as we scrambled over rocks, knelt
to capture sleeping crabs and squirming eels.

Although this place, trekked by pilgrims who come
to climb to the island's church and look at outlines
of Viking houses, is miles to the north of the one
we shared, although we've lived decades in terrains
so apart no path could link them, on this beach
I half believe the one from long ago is in reach.

Although you misread, misunderstand me – neither
of us is in tune with the other's language – I am writing
to tell you how the sea scoops shells as it sweeps
over sand, wipes out the causeway, drowns rocks
and how, in spite of the dividing water, the island
is stitched to this shore fast as finger to hand.

Myra Schneider

Year's End, Orford Quay

Brought to this brink,
white boats glazed blue,

a flinted shore
and a long dark limb,
the thousand-year
drift of the ness.

The wind honing us,
scalpel of the east,
cutting worries
and webs away

so we stand
whistle-clean
of ourselves
in strips of sharp light:

three staves
in the crisp impermanence.

Lynne Wycherley

The day I knew I wouldn't live for ever

The summer I conquer water, I taste power again
like learning to walk, but this time I'll remember –
being that proud impossible thing, a swimmer;
ecstatic, buoyed up, striking out and out,
swooping with the waves, diving through.

I flip to look back, and the beach is painting-
by-numbers – coloured patches so small I can't tell
which are my family. I was one of those bright dots
and now my space has closed behind me.
I could not exist, and there'd be no difference.

The sea starts to jostle and leer, I've swallowed
knowledge more serious than I knew there was.
This is too vast for me, and I'm swimming hard,
but the dots and patches don't get bigger. No point
shouting, I am invisible – too far out for anything

but keeping on, though without hope, with no
breath, and aching arms. But my life so far
doesn't pass before me like the teacher said, and now
my feet nudge sea-weed, and I wade, jelly-legged
and look for our umbrella, and find it.

Nothing has happened. They haven't missed me.
It's cold. My knitted swimsuit is bleeding magenta
into powder blue. My parents set up cricket stumps.
They don't know it's all the same who wins.
The sun makes them cheerful. I am so much older.

Carole Satyamurti

Estuary Island

So it was silt, sand and a fish box
washed in by the North Sea,
but it was our den all summer,
cut off twice daily, hidden by dunes.

A season of sand castles, shells,
crabs' claws, dried seaweed decorations,
the little world we made,
burning salmon poles at the summer solstice.

That last night of the holidays,
two cans of Tennent's lager
between us all, everything changing,
him and me the last to leave,

piggybacking to a windswept shore,
his hands on my thighs,
the fullness of his shoulders,
a sudden storm, marram stinging

bare skin, red weals in the morning,
the rhythm of his south-bound train,
a serenade for charred wood on the beach,
a fish box floating towards the horizon.

Fiona Ritchie Walker

Horizons

Handed to me through the blue front door
of the pebbled cottage down the steep street,
Jamie made at once for my iPad, finding his way
in seconds through a country new to me
straight for a video clip of Springtime.
So I zipped up his new blue jacket
and led him down to the quay
to take an open boat to the point
where seals breed, and oystercatchers,
and Caspian terns,
aching with love for the old mud horizons
and the racing tide, wind over the saltings
and seventy years of crabbing.
At my feet on the deck, Jamie
cuddling a black dog all the way,
a black dog licking his fingers.

Hilary Elfick

7am: Mauritius: To The Sea

Your hills are more lush than any pasture,
your crop more plentiful, your grass more green.
Each morning I smell your fringe before
opening my eyes. You salt-pique my brain
and draw me out to stamp-dance on the sand.
Each blue dawn opens with my garden
pricked out with new shells, contraband
oozing fat-footed slugs, slithy and waxen.

Sea, it is time I settled with myself.
I want your stubborn pulsing to glut my
need for cradling: to sleep and be rocked.
I want to sit on a low stone shelf
imagining breakfast, and to plait my
daughter's wind-knotted hair, lock over lock.

Marianne Burton

Tidal Bore

At first, a soft breeze blushes my left cheek
then brushes firmer, firmer still
until it pushes as hard as a bully
and I'm close to falling from this high wall.

I can smell a cargo of crabs and seaweed,
sandbanks and driftwood, diesel fumes
and death. They're being funneled
on the wavefront of an incoming tide

as if the moon has herded the sea,
chased it inland up the river.
It rolls closer, scaling its own height,
then higher until near to flying.

Its roar drowns my ears.

I'm turning to salt.

Then suddenly it's past,
leaving in its wake
a sky shrouded in silence,
a whelp-filled river

and my dizzied self,
returning
to a different kind
of vertical.

Pat Borthwick

The Evening Swim

An evening swim like any other it seemed,
The low sun, the undulating dance
Of waves, turning to gold in its soft beams,
Ripples caressed into a rhythmic trance.

One was swimming already without looking back,
Cut his own furrow, forging his path to the sun.
The watchers stumbled, eager to follow his track,
Stopped short at the shock of the water, and one by one

Looked out again to the swimmer, afloat on the ocean;
Rings and spirals of fire, unfolding and folding,
Buoyed the dark head up, and bobbed with its motion,
Spread counterpane of gold thread, sea-mountains moulding.

They drew back slowly, silent and chilled to the bone,
As the swimmer slipped on through the glitter and sparkle, alone.

Hermione Sandall

Hiatus

The wind has stopped nagging the grass,
buffeting clouds and ruffling waves,
so the sea lies back in the sun
and meditates.

Sea pinks stretch their necks.
The gorse draws in its claws
and breathes out yellow flowers.
Old stones hum.

Hidden, she watches, intrigued by how
the world gets on without her,
learns to heal itself,
clean and calm in time with the tide.

Susanna Harding

Sound of Mull

Watching the daily pilgrimage of tide
prayer the Sound from sea to sea
all colours green

I learn to grace the moment as the sun
lifts each crested wave and
fills it with white light;

the whole ragged loveliness of this world
meets my fierce tenderness,
joins in the dance,

before I turn to lean once more
into the end-of-winter wind
and land-locked days.

Elisabeth Rowe

Pier

Speak to our muscles of a need for joy
W H Auden 'Sonnets from China' (XVII)

Left at the lodge and park, snout to America.
Strip to togs, a shouldered towel, flip-flop over
the tarmac past the gangplanked rooted barge,
two upended rowboats and trawlers biding time.
Nod to a fisherman propped on a bollard,
exchange the weather, climb the final steps
up to the ridge. And then let fly. Push wide,
push up your knees so the blue nets hold you,
wide-open, that extra beat. Gulp cloud;
fling a jet-trail round your neck like a feather boa,
toss every bone and sinew to the plunge.
Enter the tide as if it were nothing,
really nothing, to do with you. Kick back.
Release your ankles from its coiled ropes;
slit water, drag it open, catch your breath.
Haul yourself up into August. Do it over,
raucously. Head first. This time, shout.

Vona Groarke

69

The Matter of Britain

The real coast's unfixed, foundering,
each tide washing off the last.
Grains and stones shift, nudging,
knocking, a vibration of edge
no map can catch.

An awkward old relative,
visited with nervous tremor.
Beyond the daily surge,
gathering in the undertow,
a giant's attack,
hacking off land limbs.
Elsewhere, fussy gifts of sand.

But family, after all –
somewhere to go,
to walk between the sea and sadness,
to slip the clutch of words,
to feed on space.
To feel your skin
thrill to the touch
of the icy, dancing edge.

Pamela Coren

an absolute universe

Those Colours

Suddenly,
in the cold grey water,
those colours –

fluorescent tubes
of natural light.
The purple, orange and green

of a turning globe,
like an extra-large marble
from childhood.

The world of a two-inch jellyfish
suspended in sea.
An absolute universe

minding its own business.
Its self-contained beauty
startling, confusing

and touching the heart
of the rainbow within me.

Fiona Durance

Hermit Crab

Down in the Causeway's green fringes of weed
Tiny crabs like pieces of jewellery – buttons, beads,
Brooches, ear-rings – scuttle, dart and feed.

Here's one. A grey-green winkle
Scrambles on knuckles
And two pairs of stilettos.

A hand, hiding in a shell.

Goggle-eyed, it grapples
Weed, food, one pincer
Raised at a rival – a foil.

At once
Solitary and countless,

Tentative and furious,

A stone-age hermit, skulking in its cave,
The curve of its shear claw
Shielding its threshold,

Around it, its black bowl
Crusted with coiled white tube-worms,

Above it, the darkening sky, with stars, with questions.

Katrina Porteous

Sea Hare

The Sea Hare slips from water-forms,
scribes patterns in sand with ivory shells

and seagull bones to light paths unseen.
She rides the storms on ribbons of kelp,

stalks waves when they covet slivers
of painted wood or steel mirrors for vanity.

She spins, with sea hare skill, tunnels that twist
and shimmer in blue, green, black; sequins

them with plankton glow to guide lost
sailors home to her green-lit halls.

The slow old river soothes to her whispered
challenge; he falls into her web of tricks,

losing each game to give up small swimmers
he would hoard in rooms of woven weed.

Angela France

Intertidal

She tells me how it lives, quick and rich, between tides;
how its world shifts in swirls and sanded patterns on each waking.

> How it scurries to take all that's offered by each new land
> exposed on the moon's whim, washed in the sea's run.

How it waits out high tides in a bubble bound with silk,
how each barnacle only has room for one.

Angela France

from **On the Beach**

Pool molluscs, marooned
by tide's swift retreat, grip,
beauty tight within.

June Hall

Sea Anemone

Soft-suckered pinkly onto jagged rock,
dreaming in swaying brine. The frothy lips
meet flesh smooth-slimed as glass. The slap and shock
of moon-pulled salt turn blossoms into rosehips.
Tight shiny buds hold firm to a craggy ledge.
As squalls turn calm, as eddies swirl away,
the fronds uncurl, explore the upper edge
of blue-lit stillness. From the shadowed bay
a rash of silver sparks explodes and turns,
in clouds of eyes and fins, to sunlit bowls
abundant with the scarlet living ferns.
The bright-knit swell of shimmering unrolls.
And, brushing rosy arms, one beating spark
is pulled, by more than moon, into the dark.

Fiona Durance

Well Drilled
Morecambe Bay

I've never seen this before, oyster catchers stretched out
in a well-drilled line as the tide comes in
the roar of its dull thunder powering the sea
that pours across flat sands.

One moment
I could've sworn all I saw was mud, but
as the sun breaks cover
to draw the bay silver, it's the tide I see
bellying in with sidewinder waves
and the birds, black-and-white waiters with orange bills
dragging it in on invisible filaments
like a table cloth
all along the edge of the sea
over flat, grey mud where waves curve
and birds scurry, actors
in the twice daily drama of drawing
the tide shorewards.

Geraldine Green

Dunlin

Last stroll from Cemlyn.
The cliff murmurs thrift
sand spurrey, sea rocket.
The sun gives them life.

A sign warns 'Bull in Field'.
I believe I heard him once –
sea-monster roar
as if he'd crawled from the Otherworld
scaled rocks
and in seep of darkness
bawled his petition to the moon.

On my knees before a miniature garden
webs of emerald moss, dove-green tentacles
of lichen, salt-wort's needled knots.
A lugubrious heron flaps by.

A blurred *sreep, sreep* and dunlin
in one chittering sweep below the headland
one body flowing – quick and sinuous
as silk georgette tossed to the wind.

The ocean bellows, sighs.
Earth's voice translates as sea couch
sage-blue air
as the violet scent of a dying sun.

Joan Poulson

Eavesdropping

Shearwaters not unlike an assembled attentive audience
have arranged themselves on a suitable rock a semi-circle
of spent match heads against a lemon sky, straight backed,
evening jackets brushed, chests plumped ready for the entry
of tonight's conductor

who won't be the young seagull air-hanging
like a wind-blown newspaper's blurry print of juvenile speckles
not interested in small black birds, still learning the art
of successful scavenging when fishing skills desert him,
the evening now so still

a slap of water from an unseen lacuna shocks the bouroch of coots
rising and falling in unison, swapping hen stories
under ziggurat-piled clouds
like that land where cuneiform was developed on clay tablets
but here broken black palings inscribed on the sky by another stylus –
an outline of shags

on a long rock, wings half stretched, folded right angles
beaks pointing to heaven, no room on their rock for the flock of
migrants
forming, re-forming their shape like a bee swarm against a draining
sky,
a trail of eider duck bobbing in astonishment ooh ooh Ooh?
gurgling;
water standing in yellow-ochre pools not yet sucked back into ocean.

Sheila Templeton

Turnstone

Bowing to its breakfast, this small bird
fossicks in a frayed coil of twine,
splitting hairs to loosen fishy dots,
rags of membrane. It disregards
the puffed oval of a pitta bread
that bowls, flips, turns itself back
into a half crab-shell, holding a spoonful
of sand like sifted flour. Sugar grains
give way to crumbs, to grit, to ridges
of stone eggs, poised to avalanche
down. Sea trundles, onshore wind
flicks the bird's feathers. It persists,
prods, gulps. The sun comes out
and every pebble has its shadow.

Christine Webb

Shoal

Herring,
muscle of the sea.
In all his stories,
you winked
like silver shillings
flipped
through tides.

All his life
you went by flashing
in your thousand
thousands,

ghosting
in your shoals,
like little planets
leaning
on the dark.

Jean Atkin

Survival

We fly together, my kind, the silver-sided.
We circle, bunch or dive in unison
a brotherhood strong in choreography.

We keep away from the branching groves
where killers lurk: the prowling shadows
and ogres launched from hidden caves.

We scorn the bottomers, flat with both eyes one side,
skulking in sand; but only the rash fly high
where two-pronged darts puncture the roof to seize us.

We hate the hard bellies farting across the roof
trailing their stinking excrement and tentacles
which trap our kind, lift us out of the world,

but most we fear the silent-flying monsters
with their triangle sails, twin-bladed tails;
suddenly upon us, spinning us into our frenzy dance
as the massive jaws and pointed tearers snap.

Jean Watkins

The Seals

There they were
at a solemn distance
like apostles

wedged
on white sand
in their sulking purples

the sea slung with weed
yet holding more light
than anything else.

Shaping spirits –
for when they had gone
we stood in the undertow

as if their music
were still perceived
through the skin.

Pauline Stainer

Leviathan

Across the sky, Leviathan,
sprung from a cleft wave
has caught the splintered sun
in a cataract of glass.
His downward plunge
through a swirl of plankton
scatters the sequinned shoals
that cruise through hidden canyons
where his shadow prowls.
The high sweeet notes call,
plead and soar, unanswered –
the harpoon trails his broken flank,
a red surf breaks.

Angela Kirby

Not Alone

have you ever had the feeling you're not alone definitely not alone
and of course you're not alone   you're on a boat with friends
in the Helford River   and the water's clear   as if it's carrying
mirror reflections from the other side of the world   and
you're glad you're not alone   lots of other boats
in this picture postcard setting are having fun like you
pottering in a gentle dying wind with a taste of the tropics in it
the sun's out   and everything's . . .
but you know you're definitely more not alone than you've ever been
there's a sense of not-aloneness that's physically stifling
your blood pressure's rising by the minute
racketing round your head till it feels like thunder
and everyone starts fidgeting   rubbing the backs of their necks
though no one says anything   and you're thinking   this started
out
as the most peaceful day in your life   so why
are you looking at each other and at the navigator
(he's the skipper but suddenly he's jumped into navigator status)
and perhaps spelled with a capital N because the river's become
a minefield of unexploded mysteries   and people in the next boat
are waving at you and pointing at the water
so you look over the side thinking you're dragging a line
and there   cruising silently along   at exactly the same speed as you
underneath you   right underneath you is a basking shark
bigger than your 24-footer   it would only take
one heave of his giant back to flip you all in the water   perhaps
he thinks your black hull is another shark   a shark in the mood for
love
and your boat has lovely barnacles at this end of the season
and other undoubted charms   and maybe she's being a bit coy
heeling over now so only one alluring flank is showing
because there's a puff of breeze and that's the only thing that's little
about this day   and still no one's said anything   only given
sharp intakes of breath   and then he's not there any more

Caroline Carver

86

Shell

Tiny shell, pearly as a milk tooth, why
did I choose you to put in my pocket?

You might be the eye of all storms.
You might orchestrate clouds,

the drift of sand, or perhaps
the oyster catchers' red beaks

prodding and probing the shoreline.
The drapery of seaweed over the rocks.

Your hollow ear might contain
sounds spiraled through Time,

some still burning and blinded
with the origin of Here.

You understand Moonspeak,
commune with the sun.

Today, your dark lid is closed
although I know you still see.

The beach wants to gather around you,
waits to hear Wise from your lips.

Little Oracle, you've reached out,
touched me. It's your pocket I'm in.

Pat Borthwick

Sea Creatures Sing

no sea without us
                we are
the white light that flickers
                in its veins
twists in the helical
          thread of water
you see us corkscrew through
                the shallows
flash cometary bling
                in blackest wall of wave
hint with a wicked little eye
        at monsters
                dream with a drift
of parachute silk in rock pools.

                we are
the trillion pearly fingernails of the sea
                its wise indifference
dark predation of shark fin
                killing flump
of a whales's tail
                myth of a mermaid's song
piano pluck
                of pebbles
oiled hinges of its movements
                weight of its flung body
disappearing
                come again of its soul

we are telling you this story
                as if we were fingerprints
on drowned wood

when we are gone
                and the sea is a wet dish of minerals
you will have to call it
                something else.

Kate Foley

that wet fist

Living Next Door to the Sea

is like living next to a man
with an unpredictable temper and a pit bull.

You smile when you see it, say good morning sea,
squinting sideways for signs
of mood change, a darkening, an unusual quiet,
the absence of birds.

Some days it's ok to walk the beach,
gathering stones, or even dip the toes.
The sea lies flat in the sun, growling in its sleep.

Other times you're grateful for the garden fence,
the space between.

Then you wonder if the fence would make
the slightest difference, if push came to shove;

or the space between mean anything at all,
under a full moon, with a spring tide,
when a tremor far away shakes the earth
and sends that wet fist
towards your little certainties.

Ann Alexander

Kleptomaniac

The sea has set its stalls
halfway along the beach.
We rummage through its bric-a-brac,
collect smoothed glass, driftwood,
unusual rusty shapes.

Snatched down from someone's roof,
sucked cornerless,
a marled and sooty stack
sunk into the sand.
Who would have thought to find this here,
brick-red symbol of the heart of home?
And close by,
a whole corner of a house,
claimed and prised away
as frightened fingers lost their grip.

Were they prepared,
the family on the sofa by the fire?
It was a familiar sound,
the hungry sea opening wide its jaws,
calling down on the tongue of the wind
into the room. Tweaking the lights.

Generations had heard it so.
Slept with it. When angry,
bellowed at each other over the top of it,
were drowned out and laughed.
The storms come closer they said,
kept saying.
Only the gardens shivered and shrunk.

Imagine that sea,
gnashing and grinding and hissing.
A great, greedy cobble-filled mouth,
world traveller in league with the wind,
defining and looting the land.

Then that house, a home,
raked down on a whim
to end gobbed at the clay cliff's back
with spittle and trash from the sea.
A kleptomaniac is stamping down this coast
I WANT! I WANT!

Pat Borthwick

*The Yorkshire coastline from Boulby Cliffs in the north through to Long Nab nearer
to Hull is collapsing into the sea. It is the fastest disappearing coastline in Europe.*

With Salt

nothing soft lasts here
the sea eats clean to the bone
a knife in each hand

Eleanor Livingstone

Making Space for Water
*Title of a Government Consultation Paper setting out their
strategy of non-intervention against coastal erosion.*

Closer than breath or pulse he hears the sea
which laps as gently as a cat, or hurls
its breakers down, arcs foam across the quay
and grinds the shingle when each wave unfurls.

His aerial snapshot shows a garden plot,
a house with smoke blown from the chimney-stack
across striped lawns, his trailer with a yacht,
the cliff, the beach and lines of tidal wrack.

All that is left him is a strip of land
and caravan. The house was undermined
by high tides scouring, sucking clay and sand
until it fell; and now he cannot find

the will to mend the dangling fence, or do
much more than prop the board that reads *Belle Vue*.

Jean Watkins

A Likely Story

'Sometimes the sea breaks in,' my grandfather said.
'You must be vigilant. Have I ever told you
the story of the man on this very marsh
in the night of the great floods, 1953,
when the tide came knocking at his own front door,
and when he opened up, a pig swam in,
grabbed him in its trotters, and carried him off,
right through the kitchen and out the back door?
Together they sailed the dark drowned lands
till at last they grounded not far from here.'
We didn't believe him. We saw the sea's obedience,
the strong arm of pebbled shore, the sleeping dykes
ribboned in sunlight; we went on hunting
ammonite and amber, launched driftwood boats,
not looking up when the wild geese flew over.

Elisabeth Rowe

Brute

They took us to the edge of the world
where chaos heaved – a huge grey beast
slavering at the sand, sucking at stones.

Aged three I knew, refused to tempt it
though my sister ran shrieking in and out
shocked by the cold, thrilled at her daring.

I can taste the salt of my father's broken promise
when he let me go, water closed its lid,
in a green element I knew electric panic.

Now we herd between flags, minded by lifeguards
mindful of its malevolence; the airbed drifted
quietly to deep water, the pincers of an undertow.

I have heard its roar, seen fathoms flung on rocks
at Hell's Mouth, Bryher, exploding in white and silver,
read of the wrecks littering Scilly's seaways.

A TV reporter on a beach points out the cliff
where a freak wave snatched two boys, or the spot
where a man trying to save his dog was drowned.

Jean Watkins

The Storm

The sea churns, rough
so two young men must swim
to their boat tied way out
bucking like the metal horse
in our playground at home
(don't mention those who fell under it – legs broken)

Fishermen tip toe the edge,
try to haul fish life from it
(don't mention hope
don't mention dark sunlight or the storm coming in)

The early cormorants are long gone,
now a family chucks stones
as if to match the heave and thrust
of the very ocean we crawled from –
stone throwing is all we have left
(don't mention evolution)

The wild sea excites us all, flags waving
people huddle with hoods up
shout to each other.
The young men have reached their boat.
Now what?
(don't mention the future)

Mist blurs the headland
soon the foghorn
will moan like a widow
(don't mention the shapes lying deep in the bay)

Rose Cook

The Monday Sea

On Sunday, like an Old Testament prophet,
the sea roared warnings
over the rusty railings of the prom.

The old penitents crouched in the shelter,
heads down; tut-tutting over
the inky Sins of the World.

The owners of insistent dogs
genuflected in the wind
until the ritual of the plastic bags was done.

How blameless the sea looks,
under the Monday sky
even though the workaday beach
is littered with the memory of the storm.

Ann Alexander

Slick

No life can breathe in its trail,
no joy survive such engulfment.
When the sun goes out,
and strings of slime crawl
through once jade-green waters,
the moon's left to weep white light
on the spilling of dreams.

June Hall

Hovercraft Accident
Ryde – Southsea 1972

Head down, a woman
shuffles along the shore,
pays no attention to the waves,
her feet pecking at the debris.
She wipes her tears
bends to gather a handful of shells,
enough for a necklace –

remembering her child
eager for the sea, a day trip,
with her uncle, a birthday treat;
recalls the wash of the ferry,
the upturned hovercraft caught
in a wall of white water –
the breaking news.

Denise Bennett

Is It the End of the World?

On the shore, the witnesses
silently muster, some gazing
out to sea, some idly picking
over seaweed and flotsam.
Those who are too tired to stand
bend stiffly down to sit
uncomfortably on cold pebbles.
A wind blows off the water;
storm clouds gather above
a lurid light on the horizon.

This is a congregation of grey
shades, sober survivors of some
tragic experience or other,
not connecting, not wanting
to be there, or to see
what is going to happen.
Almost, you might say,
ghosts in waiting. Mostly
older folk, though some young,
who should be out dancing
somewhere else, except that
something already happened to them.

Is it the end of the world?
a boy asks his grandmother.
Oh, no, she says, just another day.
We come here to pay tribute,
to watch the ships passing,
to look out on the grey sea
and wonder what we are waiting for.
Is it a holiday, then? says the boy.
Ssh, says grandma, too many questions.

The grey sea surges ceaselessly on,
pushing the pebbles in, pulling them out,
in, out, in, out, in, out.

Rosemary McLeish

Lament for an Illegal Immigrant

No moon, but fishermen
are used to that and the sea's chanting,
the descant of the nets. The decks
silvered with sea verses,
the minims and trebles of fish
hushed into songbooks of ice.

Something didn't sing, humped
in the net, thudding onto the deck.
Its ears heard no notes, its eyes
were blind to the men standing round,
its throat choked with words
that no-one would hear.

They let the sly octopus
sidle to the ship's side, forgot to stop
the arch and leap of bream.
The sea moaned, the fish
slipped out of tune, the kittiwakes
hurled screeches like broken strings.

The men unfroze, thumped
what didn't sing, what was lost for words,
over the hissing deck. Tipped what had
no hope, had never had a hope,
back to the sea. No
word, no hymn, no prayer.

But the rags of its clothes cried. The sea
beat its fists on the boat. And the wind got up
and howled till dawn.

Gabriel Griffin

Soft Engineering

Ceaselessly licking the coast
the sea is engaged in soft engineering.
She tongues up heaped, trickling spits
of shingle, as a mother cat
pridefully peaks up the wet fur of kittens.
Slick and shiny, precision smoothed
pebbles from the sea's mouth
glissade down the wave that drops them.

She is tooled up for many tasks;
not only the smoothing of freckled sands
but the saw-toothed carving of collops
from the land's edge, the spirited abrasion
of hard rock till it cuts back,
curdling the water in a mess of foam.

Relentless as mother-love
the sea builds the bone of the land
and scoops its soft, domed tilt.
But of all her multiple pregnancies,
the land will never grow up,
out of reach of that inexorable tongue.

Kate Foley

the wide horizon

Rocking Horse

The sails are asleep,
The morning air
Brushes past, like a lover, whose touch
Brings certainty, makes steady.

Slews round,
Broaches swirling, then, wrenched by the water,
Skeeters off, and gybes with a crash,
Brings all the logs rattling down;
But she keeps a steady course,
Balances across the plank bridge,
Plants the right number of steps
To clear the next jump.
And so with the boat
Tittuping over the corduroy sea
Contained and collected,
Her strength gathered up.

Look from the clifftop, it forges purposefully,
Riding its own plumb line above the depths,
With just a little nod.

Hermione Sandall

Survey Ship

Slowly, up and down,
scarcely raising bow wave
or tail wake, silent-engined
she glides, clinging to the shore
on this pass.

She too is mapping,
mapping below-the-surface
surface changes of the earth.
Not hers pen and parchment,
astrolabes or ink –
sonar, computer software
and electronic gizmos
draw her lines.

She charts unseen dangers,
shifts in rock formations,
sandbanks, exposed wrecks,
peeling layers of secret skin
from the mask of the globe.

Lyn Moir

Harbour in Winter

Frost cracks the harbour wall, a film of rime
scumbles the foreshore rocks. The sea
growls in the distance. For the time,
the wall holds firm. In its lee
a dozen fishing smacks have crept
out of the wrestle with weather. Snow
deepened around them as they slept
and now their decks are white. The row
of cottages shows here and there a light.
                    No stir
on land or in the deep green water
inside the harbour bar. A northern whaler
has put in here. Along her hawser
and strung-out rigging, icicles en masse
glitter in dawning sun like broken glass.

A C Clarke

Old Boats

There is no water in the old harbour;
The *Sea View* is a snare and a delusion.
A few old boats lie drunken and decayed
Behind the sandbar that denies them life.
This whole adventure has been a disaster:
All you had wanted was to see the sea.

I lay down by your side in the stale room
Trying to come to terms with disappointment.
Although I know I teetered into sleep
Weeping for you and me and the old boats,
I dreamed for them the return of the sea
Feeling it for them, happy in the dark.

And, Oh, the touch of it! The merry lick,
The cheeky elbowing of their underneaths
And then the bold shouldering-up of them
From the sucky clutches of the dreary mud.
Now balancing, careful at first, and then
The great tipsy surge of the communal rocking
Their timbers singing along to the tinkling of halyards
And all yelling together – *thalassa! thalassa!*

Ann Drysdale

Resurrection
Le Cimetière de Bateaux, Brittany

Don't stare – they'll stop. But once you've turned
they go on heaving free of the ria's mud. Stem,
keel and stern-post fit and fasten. Ribs expand,
feeling for the air. Spars bristling with nails
lift and turn to nestle into place. A dinghy
flips off kelp and barnacles, wraps on planks of elm
and clamps them tight. A whaler rights,
shakes out sand, laps each resinous strake
over the one below to grow its clinker skin.
Gunwales stretch from bow to transom.
Caulking packs joints as masts shoot up,
quiver to the wind. Rudders twitch and
wheels jink as canvas begins to snap.

The tide lifts them, holds them.

They can race the gale again or defy it
in lightning stitches; lull at anchor while
silver-pulsing dragnets scrape their sides,
frost their decks with scales. They'll nose
through mats of bladderwrack, feel their timbers
clench against pack-ice, play tag with dolphins.

We'll catch one, make it ours. Even ill winds
will blow us good as we steal back old lives.

Gill Learner

Baptism

Huge wheel clutched in outstretched hands
Outsized oilskins, yellow blue and white
Astonished eyes and open mouth

Feet groping the steep sloped deck
And now the grey froth flies
Catching rainbows in its arc

To pound the cheeks and smart the eyes
And shock with penetrating streams
So mouth gasps and hands fly from wheel.

Boat corkscrews, feet find new angle,
Then shouting laughter from across the deck
'You're fine, Adam, but DON'T LET GO!'

And O the thudding energy beneath his feet
As joyously she cuts into the waves
Her one permitted triangle set fore

Reined tightly by those quivering sheets
And guided by those clenched wet hands
Stretched out on the wide wheel.

Hilary Elfick

To the Lamp Room

The ferryman mentions a sharp drop
later. Troubling lack of cloudcover.
Penultimate week, he says, over
his rhythmic shoulder, before winter-
mooring her. Yes, frost, surely.

We disembark below a line of
overbright prefabs – petrol-blue,
lilac or cherry – where whin and
scrubby tamarisk shield porches.
Bleachy rose-print curtains expose
Belfast sinks, enamel basins,
cups. No letterboxes. The postvan rarely
slows for such mercy-of-the-tide outposts.
A window shelf displays a late
Clarice Cliff creamer. You pose
for a throwaway camera.
                              We've regained
our summertime hour today. On our
own this time. We climb ninety-eight
stone treads to the latticed lamp-room.
Pineapple-size bulbs, in use the year
my grandfather changed sides.
I scan recessive coastlines, nine yards
gone on a single night once. On the ferry
again the tide has changed. Light
seeps bleakly. Edges of first frost
taste the air. Two kittiwakes stand sentry
by the car wheels. The forecast gives
trouble further out. Trouble, surely.

Anne-Marie Fyfe

Crossing

The day after the storm
I crossed to the island.
The sea was high.
The ferryman,
wiry, kind, handled the boat
with care but with enough
insouciance that the waves –
flipped up by the wind
in any case – slapped heavily
against the rusted sides
and sent a flail of spray
into my salt-stabbed face.

And all the while, a cormorant,
its neck extended, sideways eye
fixed goldenly on us,
kept pace or raced beside
our small, sea-mounted ship,
swept down the narrow channel
by the swelling tide.

J A Priestman

Ghost Ship

A counterpane of gold was floating
behind Bosavern House so I scooped
you up in your nightdress and we flew
down to the cape burning
under iridescent flame.

The sharp rocks did not scare you.
Scrambling to the summit,
your eyes scoured the scythe
of the wide horizon
where the ship would appear.
White-sailed, nettled in skeletons,
black prow arrowed towards us.

Susanna Harding

113

Becoming Variable

i.

Attend to the gulls and forecasts heard in bed,
reassurance that we're safe from winter seas

where wrecks roll under the sea lanes, tilting
in the oily wash of ferries

or fathoms down, where whales slip freely
through the Hebrides.

ii.

You must have been there in the flap and crack of canvas
that Malin stitched for you in beads of ice

and worked a slanting Dog Watch while the gales
whipped North Utsire white at nightfall

and learned co-ordinates for the sight
of black ceramic water shattering on Rockall.

iii.

I imagine you counting, between Fair Isle
and Forties, a flock of shipwrecks,

when you slept. Long after you've gone,
I think of the course of your keel

on its barred-silver passage to the mackerel north
or on the coal road from Lerwick to Shields.

Jean Atkin

Rain Coming

Out in *The Mermaid*, off Land's End,
dangling for mackerel, squinting for shark,
my son turns and says, in a small, dry voice –

Rain coming.

We stretch our eyes for a long, dumb moment
over the waves which are darkening, swelling –
at rain, in a blue-black wall of wet,
massed at the eye's far reach, and closing.

And our boat, which is all about pleasure and sport,
turns tail and runs, like a child in trouble,
rocking and skittering back to the land.

We damn near make it. There's the harbour,
spreading its arms. We fling ourselves at it,

too late. The rain comes swaggering, roaring,
over the sea like a pantomime pirate,
people shouting *Behind you! Behind you!*

Umbrellas flapping, arms alarming,
skipper cussing, the engines coughing,
passengers panicking, heaving, baling,
all so wet we might have been drowning –

without knowing why, we're out and scrambling
back in our element, running for cover.
The wet, white face of my son, eyes staring,
is mouthing over and over,

Rain come.

                    Ann Alexander

Lighthouses

Pladda: 3 white flashes per 30 secs; Lady Isle: 4 white flashes per 30 secs:
Alisa Craig: 1 white flash per 4 secs. (Northern Lighthouse Board)

Tonight a milky misty sea
as if this soft grey day
is drained, funnelled to blaze
amber-rose and gold
from lichen, seaweed, old rocks;
the moon still a wispy question
in a pale sky, back-lit
by an unseen sun.
The sea has hidden its islands
Pladda, Lady Isle, Ailsa Craig,
Holy Isle – even Arran
though its peaks are reprieved –
sharpened brush strokes
of Japanese-blue,
a clue that darkness is falling;
and that from small clusters of rock
with the same certainty as sunrise,
light, white, always white
will shine; sifting
safety from danger,
solitude from loneliness.

Sheila Templeton

116

Rubh An Eun

Out on a spit of land, far as it gets
this metaphor (communication, isolation, you name it)
isn't as dead as it looks. We've walked past often,
assumed the rusting carapace must house
the ghost of a lamp, cobwebbed, cracked perhaps,
but definitely long past beaming.

Nights it beacons from the southmost tip
of the island, red-eyed stare six seconds long.
Lighthouses have their own language:
ignore them at your peril, if you're at sea.
No need to make them shoulder weights of meaning
besides that one word *Danger!*

which they faithfully proclaim, come wind,
come tide. This one, still signalling
across the narrow firth, warns fisherman
and ferry crew alike: they take it as read.
If it missed even a day, the familiar coast
would reconfigure, bearings lost.

A C Clarke

The Last Lighthouse
Shetland

Glimpse it
through wind-blown flecks,
gulls, gannets,
its shape held steady
through their snow

as north as north can go,
nothing beyond
but a pig-iron heave,
a sky clawed bare by the cold.

It stands on the brink of dream
where land must end
and the ultimate begins,
glass chasing glass.

I search the edge
for the glint of its tear,
the blink of its star,
its single repeating
flower of fire.

It burns in me now –
one diamond
held against death.

Lynne Wycherley

the constant taste of salt

On Land, He Is a Chapel Man

At sea, he wears a red scarf at his throat.
He won't wear green. He touches wood.
Never says thirteen. He will not sail on Friday.
Will not sail if he should pass a vicar, or a nun.
He cannot sail if crow or owl lights on his boat.
He never sails with Finn, or woman.
Will not talk of rabbit, pig or rat.
Carries in his coat a bone, a ring,
a piece of purple glass.
Takes nothing from the sea but fish.

> Landed, he's a chapel man,
> sings like a burly angel in the choir.
> Landed, he's a family man,
> digs his garden, mows and trims the grass.
> Landed, he's a social man,
> and likes his seven pints.

He never whistles, when he is at sea.
Had a mate once, whistled up a wind;
the sea bucked underneath them like a whale
shaking some irritation from its back
and tipped him overboard.
All the wild night they searched, crying his name.
Next day rose calm.
The skipper put a candle on a slice of bread,
floated it on the waves, to comfort him.
He thinks of this friend,
as he ties his optimistic knots,
his sheepshank, clove hitch, Turk's head, true love.

> On land he is a chapel man,
> and wishes to be buried there one day.

Ann Alexander

121

Picking the Silk
Laver collecting, Pembrokeshire

1906

They come in little groups between the tides
Moving along the wildest western beach
Lifting the torn silk from the dripping rocks
lovingly drying the salt tears of it
sending it thence to be made wet again.

1996

Around the corner, in the busy haven
The mighty Empress sails against a tide
That throws her sideways on the waiting teeth
In the mouth of welcoming harbour
Breaking her single skin, spilling her blood.
Terrified men on crazy tilting decks
Are powerless to catch the slick black cloak
That casts itself around the stricken ship
And curls sick fingers out and round and down
To curse the beach and turn the silk to scum.

2006

She stands now, looking out across the bay
Nothing but cold sea between her and Brazil
The dark is past and everything restored,
the birds, the limpets – and the precious silk
goes south again to make the bread of heaven.

Ann Drysdale

Cockle

slaked mud in my nails, salt-stung, wet sand
gritting up my denims, picking at beaked
slimy shellfish with a plastic fork, slurping
vinegar morsels by windy stalls and donkey-bells
uncounted derelict summers but now

when buried molluscs in moon-bled bays
combed raw by cormorant tides shoving
sandquakes ripping up silt-stuck channels
this way, that way, the little shells clattering
at plastic bottles, foam, sea-cack, rope-junk

make money, big money crated ice-stacked
this port and that and so bunked in caravans
in second-hand anoraks, ferried and packed
and forked out at night to sea-choke, people.

Pamela Coren

Lugging Worms at Whitby

Where sand meets shingle   that's where
us young girls go   filling our buckets with bait
for the men that go after the fish

too little for gutting   for net mending
but small fingers stiffen with cold just like big 'uns
and salt stings just the same

After the storms we hunt sand-curls
and blowholes   tracking them over the beach
popping the bladder wrack   pocketing shells

stamping our feet in tobacco-stained sea foam
our laughter swept inshore by wind
like skeetering gulls

Joy Howard

Fish Wife

Nae weddit tae the fish at a'
but impregnated, bonely-deep.

Five thoosan lassies track the fleet
a flock o' seagulls followin' the boats

hatit by low-season Southron landladies
wha tak oor fee but strip the rooms

fer fear fish-stench'd spoil guid furniture
wurmin', borin' intae wood and cloth.

Ma riddened honds are intimate wi' scales
an gills, roond staring een an guts

fingers numb, ower cauld tae feel
the lacerations o' shairp needle banes.

Nae ither wurk sae carried like a stain
untouchables in kirk, in shop, in luve:

the reek o' herrin wad imprint itsel
ontae the luver's pillow. We are set apairt.

Smokin' stink is woven tae the fibres
o' ma duds, the lacin' o' ma flesh

ma hair is sea-weed, skin is brine
ma sisters rise in phosphorescent shoals.

Maggie Butt

*Many thousands of Scots girls followed the herring fleet each year around the coast
from Scotland all the way down to East Anglia.*

Those Who Go Down to the Sea

They hardly ever cross my mind,
certainly never keep me awake
and tossing through the dark hours of the night

wondering if they'll make it
or whether this time the fury of the open seas
will overwhelm the frailty of their vessel.

Even when I eat fresh fish,
the costly silver harvest
torn from the fury of the waves,

I can continue a conversation
as if the delicacy placed before me
had been casually plucked from a bush

by a land-lubber
pausing in a cottage garden
on the way home for tea, unaware

of the raw flesh and watering eyes,
the constant taste of salt,
of fear.

Alwyn Marriage

Janet Hunter Remembers Her Man

He said, you had to be there
in the heart-thump and stars
and see the whales rise up

black and blowing through
the herring. When the sea split
with silver and

the air leapt with water
all the glitter and livewire
of herring.

You had to be there, he said,
watching water roll
like mercury

from cautious oars, the men
whispering to the gill nets
in the bows.

He said, it was the moon,
the herring love
the moon.

Jean Atkin

Cathy

'See yon hyeuk?' says Cathy.
'Yon's ma life.'
Three-quarters of an inch of steel,

Barbed at the hyeutter, bent,
It glitters
Like a jewel.

Tiny. Cathy, six stone, volatile as petrol,
Wiry, lean,
Puts on her shawl.

Pleased to see you, kettle on,
Deaf as a sharpening stone
To every sound

Except the wireless static crackle
From the boat,
A little whirlwind,

She pegs the sheets out in the back yard,
Scrubs the step, stirs the pan,
Swabs the floor –

'When Fetther hord it was
Another girl
He slammed the door.

Aye, but
He couldn't dae wi'oot dowters, ye kna.'

Cathy, bent
Beneath the creel:
Home from the mussel beds, the limpet pool;

Six stone of haddocks haa'ked aroond Reed Raa',
Husband, in-laws, tugging at her, kin
Needing her care,

Mussels to skeyn,
The boat to launch, lines to bait, claes to poss,
Sons to bear;

Cathy, bent with pains,
Years; busy as a sanderling,
Never still,

Down the harbour with the barrow, eyes
Blue as the Coquet, bright
As steel,

As hard, as sharp, as necessary
As a fish-hook
To the house, the men;

Cathy, without whom
A coble could not go to sea – as vital to it
As diesel, or the wind.

Katrina Porteous

Claes: clothes; *dowters:* daughters; *fetther:* father; *haa'ked:* sold from door to door; *hyeuk:* hook; *hyeutter:* the barbed end of a hook; *poss:* to beat clothes in water with a stick to wash them; *Reed Raa':* Red Row, a former colliery village in Northumberland; *skeyn:* to shell, as mussels and limpets for bait for long lines. Women traditionally baited 1,400 hooks a day for each long line.

North

1 *Kallebua*

All day and night the sea ceaselessly
casts its great, green-blue nets
under mountains thin and hard
as salt cod, as fishing folk.
They have to be hard – that's how
they all survive, winter
after winter, so far north.

We laze where rowers slumped
exhausted in their snipe-legged
rorbuer, on bunks of board
high under stone shingle, turf or tin
while weather and labour
slowly shrivelled them, like stockfish
twisting on their gibbets.

2 *Å i Lofoten*

Awe is the word
as you arrive where
the one road simply
comes to a stop
and there's not even
a track or path onward
through the chaos of rocks
and rough ground.

You walk out
across hummocky turf
away from the campervan-
cluttered car park
into a skyful of quiet. Your eye
walks the spine of the cliff
to where the final vertebra
of the stegosaur's tail

dislimns in sunset. The last
abandoned hamlet is hidden
down there, and beyond
is nothing but sea –
orcas and deeps,
the Maelstrom, blue
legends, crosscurrents
to rip a rower's arms off.

Stevie Krayer

Rorbu – shoreside wooden cabin for 'rowers', as Lofoten cod fishermen were known. Most of these cabins are now holiday homes.

The Ditty Box of Thomas Gilbert Hunter Aiken

That he left Church Closs
and his mother and stowed
away on a Tyne collier
at thirteen, dodging on board
in the wash and blow
of Lerwick harbour.

That sometimes he ate
ships biscuits so maggoty they
shuffled across his plate. That he sailed
round the Horn. That he shivered
one winter on a vessel held ice-bound
for weeks in the Baltic.

That he was wrecked
in the tide-race of Ushant, rescued
by a brig bound for Cuba and dropped
at the mouth of the Tagus to row
under Torre de Belem
into white-paved Lisbon.

That in Valparaiso he
punched a man and knocked him
overboard and then
jumped in and saved him.
That he married twice but no-one
ever mentioned the first time.

That he had a strong face, a trim beard
and fierce eyebrows. His eyes look far
past my shoulder. That we know this
from a photograph. And also have his telescope,
his drawing instruments and his cut-down,
hacked-about charts table.

That he lived to see his sons survive the War
and held his grandchildren, as babies.
That his sextant and the ditty box went missing
at last, in the bombing of Liverpool
in 1940. That he never
went back to Lerwick.

Jean Atkin

The Wisdom of the North Norfolk Crabber

'You got ter respect the sea,'
the fishermen says; he
is as much at home in the deeps
as he is on land. Keeps
a leg as it were in each.
Unlike the crabs he lands –
all glittery carapace
and clumsy, warlike assemblage
of legs – the fisherman
knows where he stands.

Sally Festing

The Ship's Gardener

I tend the garden on deck
while under the keel
forests of kelp
multiply.

Melons, love apples, aubergines –
so far from land
I have to pollinate
with a paintbrush.

Exhausted birds blow in
and sip from the nectar spurs
until an archipelago
opens in their throats.

Pauline Stainer

From Cove to Cove

Polpeor's desolate now: warped doors, cracked
concrete, rust. Once men with tides in their blood
came running at the call of bells, dared the path
against the gales, dropped to hands and knees
on the bend where fierce air clawed at so'westers,
bellowed oilskins and tried to sweep them to
the stones below. They pushed out wooden boats,
strained oars against the surge or battled to hoist
canvas while the wind fought back. They salvaged
crews and passengers from ships – *Hansey, Suevic,
Socoa* – their hulls ripped open on the Lizard rocks.

***

We're on the gallery to watch a practice 'shout'.
Bright in lifejackets and drysuits, men and women
are brisk about their tasks. The Rose grumbles
on the slipway till a whistle shrills, then glissades
until her bow bursts the shining blue. It's safer
on this side: Kilcobben's waves roll in untorn and
Atlantic fury has been tamed by fields and walls.
The boathouse curls its timber roof over all the aids to
soul-saving this century can devise. We let out our breath,
stoop to track manoeuvres through the open doors:
that vermilion will be visible for miles.

Gill Learner

the tide which will come

Going Back

Shore turf tugs at the old boat
a slow careful pulling in
grass and wild flowers
spread through the ribs
prow and stern only mind-held
salt bleached shape lines

The sea comes in for you
swirls through the sand pools
each small wave-scour
gentling you out with the tide

In this place you stay with me
shaped by the sea that you loved
and the tide is that same tide
which will come for all of us

Joy Howard

Memorial Benches, Treyarnon Bay

These headlands cannot bear
the weight of such significance:
'She loved this place.'
Can't carry so much longing.

Houses yearn for the sky,
their balconies grab at air;
and love's litter, set in concrete,
stares to sea: joy caught

behind the knees, set rigid,
to seat empty air.
'Rori's seat.' 'Debbie, fond memories.'
'Enjoy this view. He did.'

Cliffs sigh and buckle
skitter with tossed birds
wrinkle wind-scarred shoulders
then slip and twist, spiral

sighing beneath the sea;
shrinking from grief's
insatiable greed.

Pat Simmons

Undercurrent

Today the sea lags like the flap of a tired dressing gown
and a thin leg sticks out from under the waves,
blankets ripple under cover of snow-capped mountains –
where you might have been or could be in days to come –
that final battening down's left me anchorless
in this harbour where others sink or swim.

Yesterday, the surfer said, white horses rode the scene,
furious waves searched for you but their task is useless.
Simple words, *You've gone*, that's all there is to it.
No amount of staring at seagulls resting on torn masts
or listening to the plaintive cries of oyster-catchers
will bring you back, and I knew all those years ago,
Penarth Pier, walking, eating ice creams,
you singing *I do like to be beside the seaside*
I knew this day would come. Would go.

Wendy French

Tidal

Calculating the mathematics of waves
must in theory be possible. Gulls plane,
skim, contest the edibility of salt
scraps. You'd pitch stones, make them skip:
the past hands me these unconsoling
records of our lives. All this while
wind scours, brine etching on my face
new lines that burn with my loss of you –
your love of movement, love of the sea, your love.
Breakers roll in, to write on the sand
tideswell, wrecked trails of shell; still more
breakers roll in, to write on the sand
your love of movement, love of the sea, your love –
new lines that burn with my loss of you.
Wind scours, brine etching on my face
records of our lives – all this, while
the past hands me these unconsoling
scraps. You'd pitch stones, make them skip,
skim, contest. The edibility of salt
must in theory be possible. Gulls plane,
calculating the mathematics of waves.

Christine Webb

142

Ashes

The tide comes in; the tide goes out again
washing the beach clear of what the storm
dumped. Where there were rocks, today there is sand;
where sand yesterday, now uncovered rocks.

So I think on where her mortal remains
might reach landfall in their transmuted forms,
a year now since I cast them from my hand
– wanting to stop the inexorable clock.

She who died by her own hand cannot know
the simple love I have for what she left
behind. I could not save her. I could not
even try. I watch the way the wind blows
life into slack sail: the stress of warp against weft
lifts the stalling craft, pushes it on out.

Paula Meehan

143

Julia's Doves
i.m Julia Casterton

we reach the long-planned
rendezvous and find you gone

we search for your doves
but they are nowhere to be seen

there is only the grief of gulls,
the scent of pine, the hot sun

and white-fingered waves
clawing at the rocks

instead of a wreath
we pick these flowers

the small wild flowers
of Finisterre –

yellow bell-flowers, gentians
wild thyme, white campion –

and cast them out to sea, watch
as the wind lifts and scatters them

towards the Atlantic horizon
like birds, like butterflies, like poems.

Angela Kirby

Sea Song

I take off my watch, see last summer's sunshine
printed on my arm. I am still the small girl
in a trance, trailing a net along the plashy sealine,
as a fossil shell is imprinted on rock.
I crooned tunelessly, firm ribbed sand on my soles.

Now everything shifts like the sea,
that may dandle me, toss me treasure or wrack,
will overwhelm me.
The dead like seabirds throng round me.

Jo Peters

Shoreline

No-one I know has walked along this shore.
I pursue no memory, meander in the weed and spume.
The sea shouts onto the beach, tells me tales
Of those whose words were drowned, in a language
I cannot understand, not even when it writes the words
In wrack and shell upon the sand.

Gabriel Griffin

145

6, Sloop Lane

In a night air thick with low tide
and shadows of long-ago children
I trace that holiday-let among blind
alleys stepped up from the harbour.

I want you to know that the house
is smaller than I remember
an ill-fitted screen door and withered
Chronicles, a flat tube of glue
among flies on a teak windowshelf.

Promenade hotels echo too few residents.

But you'd still know the out-of-hours dentist's
close by on the hill where I fretted with an abscess,
the gents' outfitters where we found
the stormcoat that never quite fitted.

I want to tell you every last
tang-laden, mast-clinking bit of it
but even if I could mail you
or waken the dead call-collect
you'd want to know what
in this world I was talking about.

Anne-Marie Fyfe

At Borve Cemetery, 2010

'An ataireachd bhuan, cluinn fuaim na h-ataireachd àrd.'

After all this time, a bleak day for it:
rain coming down, a grey veil
over sea and machair and sky.

Once, not far from here, you showed me
the position of St Kilda. Nothing beyond
until America, you said. A fact for a child to hoard.

I don't like to think of you in this exposed place,
the Atlantic surge on eternal loop, gravestones tilting
from westerlies, the slow salt-scour fading

of identity. Your slab needs work. Strangely,
the man for it happens to be here today, and yes
he'll see to it...

We stand for a while in small-talk;
above our heads, a kittiwake is keening
into the wind.

Maggie Rabatski

147

Only a Gas
for my grandfather

                              For you,
early meant early, hours before
the crowds, the dog walkers, even
before the cleaners in their white vans,
with their rubber gloves, their tongs
for picking up dog turds, used condoms,
dead gulls.
                              To honour you,
I am early. Set out on the sand for no one
in particular, a folding chair – not too damp
to sit on – blazes canvas flowers. Here
amongst the reeds, waist-high, near clumps
of dusky sea cabbage, I can look out
to sea.
                              Before me,
an identikit slate of pewter, the sky and water
touch, as if smeared against one another by a clumsy-
fingered giant. Only the outline of a ship breaks
up the horizon. I am cold as I always was before
the fog would lift on a sunless day.

                              You are not
here with your rough white towel, stuffing lambs'
wool in your ears before you swim, your red
trunks flapping around blue-veined thighs,
the wicker picnic basket at our feet. I am hungry
for Swiss on rye, for peanut butter on white.

                              You are not here
to breathe in the smell of brash salt air, raising
your great nostrils to the sky, turning to tell me
it's only a gas that comes from phytoplasm,
the tiny plants that are the base of the ocean's
food chain, or about the floating scum that etches
fjords – a map with secret meanings. Dog walkers
are arriving; it is too late to learn.

Wendy Klein

148

Lost at Sea

A herring gull tears
on a roadside rabbit
at Lunabister.
Thin islands blow
like streamers off
the coast.
The custodian at Boddam
looks past me for
his view of voe
and surnames lost
at sea. Invisible
from here, in haar,
Garthsetters and Mansons,
Leasks and Mouats.
There used
to be Aikens at Ness,
Aikens at Ellister.
Once they were on Burra-Isle.

I'm reading graves at Papil.
Rub tough rain of lichen
off grey stone. 'William
Aiken who with crew
was drowned
March 12th 1866.'
I straighten up to find
the view his widow had:
the stones, the green,
the graves, the grazing
sheep. Invisible
from here, the sea
is sweeping up the voe
between the Burras.

Jean Atkin

The Lonely and the Sea

We don't sleep well, we who've been left alone.
Fearing intruders, we lie stiff as bone
and listen to the creak of a floorboard,
a joist. We clench our teeth against a world
deemed hostile. But then, trying to relax,
we concentrate on safe sounds: rain, or the clicks
of the battery clock; we put our tongues
behind our top teeth to release our jaws;
we switch the radio on for company;
we get up at four to make tea.

Some of us, feeling lost in large houses,
move to smaller ones near our families,
or near our best friends, or in the country,
or closer to the town, or by the sea.
And maybe this last is just what we're seeking.
For won't the waves, in their rising and falling
and withdrawing their watery weight to rise
and fall again, and rise, and fall, and rise…..
breathe like our old loves come back from the dead
to sleep beside us, here, in bed?

Janet Loverseed

claiming the ocean

Painting the Sea

Of course I haven't got to get it looking like the sea. It's my response to the sea that I want. Julia Ball

In Micronesia the sailors' charts
are made of lashed-together stalks of cane
showing the winds and currents of the sea,
and cowrie shells are islands, threaded on;
the sea as latticework, the memory of its tides
fixed in an intricate pattern of sticks.

And the painter lays down her version
of the waves and swell, the rubbed horizon
with its layers of colour through which tiny flecks
of buried pigment glint and quicken,
catching a sense of the lightness, the heart's lilt
as you enter into that expectant landscape.

with its sudden alteration in the light,
the whitening of the sky, its opening up
as you travel over hills to Monreith Bay
and see already in your mind the pink-streaked rocks,
the papery flowers of thrift beneath the cliffs,
and the sea itself, a paleness in the west –

and then you're facing something calm and limitless
that lets you stare for hours,
placed as you are in the littoral
inside the painting and beyond it,
between the burnished texture of the surface
and the wake of the memories it trails.

Elizabeth Burns

Sea Change
after *White Surf, Machrihanish*, painted by William McTaggart

The way the sea boiled that morning
should have been warning enough –
my palette laden with Titanium White
so it tilted towards my thumb
with its weight. Just as, hours later,
the whole sea tipped from West to East
so fast, roller raced over roller until
the ocean built itself into a wall
blotting out sky darker than Payne's Grey.

Then, with its racehorse tongue,
it gulped down the shoreline, seawalls,
promenades, amusement arcades,
ice cream parlours and, behind them,
offices and houses, even the church
(where someone said the last they saw
of the priest was this tiny black figure
clinging to one of the bells
in the tower). The skyline gone.

They found me later in the week
under thousands of others
washed up miles down the coast –
a human raft among splintered homes,
fishing boats moored inland
riding a tide of rooftops and trees.
They said my wrist and sleeve
were smothered in white
as though I'd become half angel.

Pat Borthwick

154

Grey Forms – (1922)
from *Kandinsky Sequence*

Seals: the beach welcomes them,
tucks them into its summits of colour,
deep palettes. Now they gather
their possibilities, unravel old terrains,
rookeries bustled with meetings, reunions –
searching for continuities, fullnesses that
instinctively, they have claimed for aeons.
It is late. They know the oceans have
darkened, that seas are warming,
turning the hours against them.

Long ago, they learned to love colour,
to pull themselves up on it as they
circled the rip and swell of waves,
believing the ocean was theirs.

Katherine Gallagher

155

Turner Is Lashed to the Mast

I did not paint it to be understood
but to show how the water
makes the wind visible,
how the sea strikes
like a steel gauntlet

I scent the blizzard
lashed like Odysseus,
the air laced with diamond,
salt-pearl at my wrist

indistinctness is my forte
a gauze backdrop,
a ship hulling
to the hiss
of the vortex

I would fix
such sirens,
before unseen currents
disperse their dissolve.

Pauline Stainer

On the Sailing Boat
after Caspar David Friedrich

So on the prow the lovers lean,
She in red velvet, he in green,
Their hands clasped, hot and keen.

Their eyes stare into painted sun.
Who guides the sheltering sail? No one.
Their trip has just begun.

I would rush in, knot the line firm,
To hold them in the glittering storm,
Wrap narrow shoulders warm.

Oh, if you make it, you must land,
Find bills, lost jobs, misunderstand
A child hot in your hand,

And then another. Will you fail?
But look, the sea sleeps, still and pale.
First teach them how to sail.

Alison Brackenbury

Landlocked

after *Landlocked* by Maggie Taylor

I was trawled inland
when they drowned the fleet
in foreign fish
and mother fetched up
off Flamborough's coast,
in father's fishing gansey.

Freshly landed
at the end of the line
I found work in the waves
and ripples of ploughed fields,
learned the moon's earth names,
milk, egg, hunter's, seed.

Frost nibbled at my feet.
My muck marked fingers
forgot the knots they knew,
became stiff with stupidity,
yet I could sing like a skylark
and bark like a rutting stag.

I'd spend days with my face
turned up to the rain,
wondering at its softness,
its lost sting,
listening for a splash,
for the echo of an ocean.

I bought these shells
from the charity shop of the RNLI,
wire them over my ears.
I cannot hear the sea.

Lesley Ingram

158

Hearing Your Words
for Ruth Bidgood, reading in Aberystwyth

I used, as a child, to imagine my death, or rather
beyond it. A ship setting out, in flames, at dusk,
counteracting the planet's roll, on the sunrise path
to a waveless far horizon lit from beneath.

This came to mind, just now, clicking on close-up
through the café window – sea meeting the sky,
distantly smooth, arching up, high above
a jumble of chimneys and roofs backlit at sundown.

I found myself catching my breath, gravity's curve
seen through such a small frame, from here where we sit
with our cups of tea. Vastness out there, our past.
But on planets elsewhere, other seas, other lives beginning.

Later, among the books, hearing your words,
it was waves I thought of – from land we may never see
reaching across the bulge of this little earth
to break, not one the same, on familiar shores.

Anne Cluysenaar

At the Very Edges of the World
Photographs by Thomas Joshua Cooper exhibited at Tate St Ives

From real to reproduced is twenty steps
but a mile of difference: from watercolour
flux & flood to anchored monochrome,
ocean moods stalled by the shutter's wink.

Diffusions onto paper with a warming
of selenium freeze the wind's flurry,
the waves' translation onto shallow shelves:
spill & plunge in uprush & swash.

From far past rote – Sole, Plymouth,
Lundy, Fastnet – fathom-black seas oscillate
across the Atlantic fetch, collide with ramparts,
collapse on sunset beaches. Reptile rocks
heave up, unchanged for centuries
but through millennia, hammered
and milled into islet & peninsula.

The Gulf Stream slides over rift & ridge
uncoiling from twenties' latitudes, past Scilly,
over Lyonesse, to ease the air
of Cornwall and the Western Isles.

From these extremes, stare across Rockall,
Malin, Hebrides; watch the trains of waves
imprinted with stark narratives; listen
for the ricochet of technology and tongues.

Gill Learner

Sea Battle
after Kandinsky 1913

There was a moment
after the sinking of the boat
when there was silence as
we reached the bottom of the sea

there was a moment
when the storm gave us back the sky
and the clouds sent down gifts,
cerulean, blue-green, ice-blue,
crimson, purple, gold, indigo,
and men became like singing seals
claiming the ocean for themselves

we sang in that moment
and the sound held fast against the light
tiered with the water's turquoise
men floated up like single flowers
while synaesthetic angels
plucked music, orange, lemon,
tastes at the edge of honey

when the storm came again
I was alone with the self
in the dark ocean of my soul
wretched, but rising still

Thelma Laycock

La Cathédrale Engloutie
Debussy / Ceri Richards

Undersea
off Brittany,
thunder.
Patches of red cobalt,
broken strings;
stone flows
between nervous intervals.

The heart picks up a surge, drops.
Salt softens things, leeches this into that.
The current drives inshore: colours spread,
brushstrokes slice into the depth.

I want the music again, but not yet,
it's too strong, shifts the roots,
powders stone. Ending makes silence,
complete things from broken.

I wait to break again,
to handle the fragments.
Make these small accumulations
which sit so curious in the tide,
run up these dangerous scales.

The call comes through the keyhole
and something to the back of me runs
to struggle with the sticky door.
What is out under the restless land
changes, changes: massive towers move
note by note, seep of pigment, surf-roar.

Pamela Coren

La Mer
On hearing Debussy at the Proms

The first tentative rays
      trace the water's surface
            pale beams
                insubstantial
          nudge against my skin

fine brush-strokes of broken light
      touch the wet canvas of the sea
          explore the water
            darker
          more troubled beneath

in the rhythm of the undertow
      the seething swell of the waves
          forms treacherous layers
              as the sea opens its raging mouth

              I am dragged close-hauled
          in the fury of the storm
        caught in the climax
     of the tempest's frenzied finale

briefly a silence

      then the gale
          of tempestuous applause
             lifts me resisting from the wreckage
             and hurls me drowning
                into the dry-dock of reality

Sylvia Fairley

Concerto

I write only the music I hear within me   Rachmaninov

in the deeps a slow to and fro to and fro
rocks the long swells into watery hills

lumbering landward   a rush onto beach
where frost catches spray on the wave-crest

and droplets of ice from the far north
rasp on pebbles like hail on glass.

Earth wakes   cold lungs breathe out a long wind
white waves thrash at dark sky

and far below   the continuo   a slow
to and fro to and fro   the pulse of us

the swell and the surge of the sea
in the blood of a born-and-bred inlander

Joy Howard

164

Another Time

come to Crosby for a fella one says
and another *what shall we call this one*
Charlie   don't like Charlie   Henry
I'd rather have Charlie

along a three kilometre stretch of strand
a hundred cast-iron figures face the sea
gaze into the westering sun
and we are here gazing at them

we stroke their mottled toadskin shoulders
drape arms round for photographs
pat heads which seem to pulse
in the afternoon warmth

brilliant but I don't like those nipples
someone says *they're weird*   it's true
they're bolts the size of matchboxes
though speaking of nipples

nothing wrong with all these Anthonys
we're delighted with them of course
but where are the Charlottes
Henriettas   where are the Antonias

with their backs turned to the land
facing their yearnings out to sea
baring their cast-iron selves
to wind and salt water

after paddles and cups of tea
we get the coach home
but we've left our other selves
back there gazing out beyond the tides

Gina Shaw

165

And beyond the garden Gilgamesh saw the sea

At first, it was simply
a sense of gaze,
moonstone so smooth
he could have sculled across

then phosphorescence
where the fish spawn,
a shift of the shining reach
like a flute underblown

and beyond, rip-tides
flashing the sun,
the assuaguing spices
on the salt-laden wind
specific as pollen.

Pauline Stainer

something in the blood

Wanting It To Be Sea

I've never lived in a house with prospect.
Just a triangle of sky, framed by rooflines,
a midland blank, but a moment ago
some trick of light made out the sea.
The house drew back, the land stretched,
and before the estate slid back,
someone inside had surged forward to look,
said *make it happen*. But it's December,
the wind's cutting its ice, no-one's going out.
Any coast would be Iceland, Novia Scotia,
Norway, the North-west passage.
My skin shivers at it. I've lost the knack.
I hear of others, family, taking the ferry to Man,
to Northern Ireland, and back and back again.
Listening in on ship to shore. Visiting lighthouses.
Gazing, always. There's no old sea-blood here,
miners, millhands, skivvies all the way
but maybe the tonnage of this middle land,
its null inheritance, conspires this need
to watch what moves as it pleases,
to take a rapid footing on the sand,
not to be scared of being late for work,
not to ask if it's allowed,
and after two hundred years
shifting other people's dirt
something in the blood wants salt
and all the weather opened out for fight.

Pamela Coren

169

The Price of Gutted Herring

She found it while searching for traffic news,
risking taking her eyes off the road
to drift between stations, would remember
the next morning that somewhere
between Five Lane Ends and Old Man's Bottom
Newcastle waned and Scotland conquered again.

A cheery voice told of upturned hay loads in Carmyllie,
broken lights in Bearsden and a main road closed
in Kirkintilloch, while she was heading to Catton
and Corbridge and queues on the Western Bypass

but for now, she was pulled in where the signal was strong,
head in hands, listening to the price of gutted herring
and catches unloaded everywhere north and west of there

on cobbled harbours glistening with fish scales,
where men with mobile phones and lilting voices
bid and bid again for cod and mackerel

and all the spoils of the sea that she remembered
miles inland, licking salt tears from fingers,
starting up the engine, trying to keep tuned in until
the voice faded and Radio Newcastle took over again.

Fiona Ritchie Walker

The Conference Hall and the Sea

They used to think that oysters opened to the moon,
bathed in its beams, captured pearls of light.

Here in the conference hall, the eager lap-tops
open one-by-one, like oysters hungry for the moon,

relaxing in the silver-dark and, as they chime to life,
an image of the sea floods onto each

its blue and soothe laps screen to screen,
until the hall's awash with aqua: underwater pool,

a lake of liquid light, as if our watery bodies crave
the element we swam from, parched for its cool embrace.

Eyes rest on distance, where the sky swoops down
to touch the waves, netting pearls of calm

before the tide sweeps out across the sand,
before the words inch in, before horizons shrink

and dock within four walls, before we close like clams,
adapt to dust-dry air and breathe.

Maggie Butt

Sightings

My dreams of the sea
are never wholly peaceful.
It beats at my front door.
I glimpse it in between
long lines of houses,
at the ends of streets
that I can't ever reach,

or else it's black, uneasy,
heaving closer underneath
a starless, moonless sky
and I have perfect sight
to see its emptiness,
the long horizon over which
no scudding sail will come.

And yet it draws me.
It is always more, and better
than my waking life. The dead
are there and young, and in
the best, unshadowed dream
I'm running on a sand-hot
shore to meet them, where
the sun is perfect morning
and the night has gone.

J A Priestman

Saying Sea

You never expected to be afraid
of losing ground.

A buzzard is waiting for you,
a juvenile, not fully grown.

When it reaches full wingspan,
it'll be time.

You couldn't say ocean, it was too grand,
so you said sea, which was immense enough.

You'd like to think of a mirror
held up, sun scattering, ripples

left in warm sand
but you imagine gravel, sharp grains

fired by wind. Above a cliff
the bird tilts, the shadow

of its wing is an oar.
Remember the first time you sat in the round,

the day the actors visited. They were dressed
as the sea, green weeds

over bare legs and arms,
faces blue, how you wanted

to be caught in the net they threw
but had no words anyone could understand.

Maria Jastrzębska

The Idea of the Atlantic

i. At the bottom of the ocean is a road
    on which the figures of those
    who will drown must walk.
    Those who see them will never forget
    their faces that are so intent,
    unmoved and perfectly innocent.

ii. If you are the girl on the ship coming home,
    this is not your home you are sailing to.

iii. And if once you look down, you are lost.
     Nothing can keep you, or call you home.
     You will be pulled deeper and deeper
     in a knot of waves. When your hands
     catch at shadows, they are ash,
     your skin a mesh of dust.
     Though the waves break open,
     and you grapple with air, you are lost.
     This sea will not be swayed by memory.

iv. What you hear when you look down
    is the noise of your death closing in.
    Listen. You could call it darkness.
    They know what darkness is,
    these road-bound shadows,
    an element, a purpose, a release.

v. Turn back from the hand-rail. Nothing is lost.
    Land is in sight and you will be safe.
    Keep away from the water's edge.
    You should know you are destined
    for a land-locked home.
    And if only the trees will be still,
    the gulls not fly so far inland,
    you will make peace with the dark,
    and need have no fear of the storm.

Vona Groarke

Sea Facing

I must down to the sea again, the lonely sea and the sky John Masefield

In my first wild waking,
behind the curtains
the sea waits: a slice of light,
the rope-pulls, their tassels,
an explosion of dust disturbed,
the impossibility of sleep. Down
a corridor of sun to the cobbled shore
I remember how everything begins
with water: the womb dance,
the last safe swim; the first hint
of drowning, the amniotic rush
of morning.

Wendy Klein

She Longs for Sea Fret

and those nights wrapped
in the small room five fields from the coast
when you could see no further than the laburnum
or the wall with the sometime gate.

Those nights with the foghorn sounding though the gauze
and the muted chant of a train escaping south
and parents just beyond the hardboard wall,
white bubbles of anaglypta that her fingers
still recall – bubbles that never burst.

And while those cold coves beneath the cliffs
were laying themselves open in the darkness,
to sea spray and an audience of stars
she lies curled into herself like the cowrie,
white and smooth, picked from the sand at Marsden
before that surge of waves that split the rock arch.

And what if the cotoneaster under the bay
window reaches up and up until it's holding
the thorned stems of the pink rose that has spurned
the trellis? And the ivy, not satisfied with smothering
the red brick wall by the kitchen, slithers across
the flat roof of the porch. The mermaid and the maygold
follow their lead and creep across the tiles
to meet the plaited creepers from the west
shedding their petals in a heap that in a fairy-tale
would be spun into the stuff of dreams.

The one she can recall, the one that came back
night after night, played out in the space between
the houses, behind the double gates.

There was a stranger generating sparks – and fire
was threatening as they swirled and struck..
She saw the stars orange against the sky – Orion's belt
was tightening round her throat, the only constellation
that she knew. The Plough was somewhere
over the grainy sea which frothed and raged
spewing its waves against the Cat and Dog Steps
(where hundreds went to soak up weekend sun)
sucking the waters from the undertow
of the shelf beside Trow Rocks.

But the black bolts hold fast.

Kathryn Daszkiewicz

Sometimes I Long for Dry Land

Bag of blood,
twisted up with
red and blue knitting.
Heart, dumb fish,
sieving through its gills
deep indigo tides, red rapids.
Nothing separate
like leaves.

Even my bones
slip sideways,
red-washed, wet.
Not like the light
dry-point scatter
of bone from the
ocean-renouncing dead.

And my brain's,
pea-princess refusal
not to be rock
is fretted by
surf and sea-weed.

I sway in my own tides,
that brassy paradox
bell in my throat
needing the opposition
of water to ring.

Kate Foley

The Sea Inside

Into a different element
We pull from the stony quay.
A chill wind breathes warm land away
And the uncertain sea,
Rippling light into darkness,
Dark into light, sets free
Rhythms that rock our boat and ropes
And shift us restlessly.

'There's nowt t' dae but wait, man.
There's nae fish.' Charlie scans
The empty miles. Why do I feel
Unsheltered, far from land?
Beyond, the Cheviot crouches,
Black Dunstanburgh withstands
The waves, the years; between them reach
The sea, the sky, the sand.

This is our forebears' country:
So the cold wind moans.
The stink of ware and salt on the fingers
And, in the bones,
The rush and heave of water,
Unknowable, unknown –
This is the sea inside us.
It rolls us round like stones.

Katrina Porteous

179

Stranded

and anchored in a fretwork of foam
over sea-shimmering silver gilt sand
I'm bliss-basking like an old grey seal
beached and loving it

so till the seventh wave
lolls over me and nudges me back
to the sea let your hands glide
over mounded flesh and soft pelt
while you plumb my fathomable eyes
and marvel at my stillness

believe me
I'm more graceful in water

Joy Howard

My Second Life

No desks and screens for me: but tanned
a biscuit brown, eyes creased from staring
out to sea; my dreadlocked hair bleached
straw by salt and sun; a wet-suit skin tight
as a seal's; body of muscle and hope.

My second self won't care about the cold shock
of the sea as long as surf is up: I'll breast
the breaking waves, buffeted and drenched,
cough water, coming up for more,
feet numb, ready for the moment and the rush.

And in the evening, salt-lipped, sand-caked,
sit by firelight, watch the sparks soar star-wards,
listen to the songs and poems of the world,
all searching for the perfect word
the perfect wave, to carry us ashore.

Maggie Butt

The Rocks

Like ocean creatures surfacing for air
we claim the light, but the jealous seas
swallow us into their vast darkness.

Who will care for us the way we hunger for?
Deep currents drag us further and further
till we become strangers even to ourselves,

shifting like waves whose onwardness
is all illusion: only at the very edge
do they race towards the waiting rocks.

Elisabeth Rowe

The Way Freedoms are Dreamt

I have purple hair in the dream –
purple hair, and I am standing
in full sun, tipping my head back.
This is familiar,
the way strange is familiar.

One of these crow-flecked days,
I will run fast down the road
right into the sea. Leave behind
the houses, with their pockets of dust,
their sleeping cats, the people with their
so-many different faces and needs
until there is only the sea,
no cupboards, no lists,
nothing to remember at all
just the roar of it to absorb
the echo and rumble that keeps
larger time than a clock,
the wash that cleans to the bones
so there is nothing left
but an again-beginning joy.

Only the turn of waves, the spread
of spilt cream, the heave and arch,
gathering in preparation to dive.

Rose Cook

the oldest dream

The Lifeboat Shed
RNLI Aldeburgh

It's that time, mid-autumn: an oil-base blue sky –
pebbles, rocks, a foothold for seagulls.
Clouds buckle, scoop grey on grey, mirror
the colours of the stones. Now, rose-tinged
the clouds fire up – a final show
before darkening. The boatshed stirs,
tugs on its moorings, flags down the breeze
as rows of street-lights flick on.

People shuffle by, shaped by anoraks, adrift
from the pack. They peer through the windows
of the lifeguards' shop, lined into
the oldest dream, of being saved
no matter what sea.

Katherine Gallagher

Index of Poets

The Poets

Ann Alexander has published three collections of poetry: *Facing Demons* (Peterloo Poets), *Nasty, British & Short* (Peterloo Poets), and *Too Close* (Ward Wood). She has won various prizes, including *Mslexia*.

Jean Atkin works as a writer and educator, and lives in Shropshire. Her first collection, *Not Lost Since Last Time*, was published by Oversteps Books in spring 2013.

R V Bailey's publications: *Course Work* (Culverhay Press, 1997), *Marking Time* (Peterloo Poets, 2004), *The Losing Game* (Mariscat Press, 2010), *Credentials* (Oversteps, 2012), and with U A Fanthorpe *From Me To You*, (Peterloo/Enitharmon, 2007).

Denise Bennett has an MA in creative writing and runs poetry workshops. She is widley published and her collection *Planting The Snow Queen* was published by Oversteps Books in 2011.

Pat Borthwick runs the Rural Yorkshire Stanza Group for the Poetry Society. Twice awarded a Hawthornden Fellowship, her poems are widely published in magazines and through competition successes. She has three full collections.

Alison Brackenbury's eighth collection, *Then*, is published by Carcanet Press (2013).

Carole Bromley has published two pamphlets (*Unscheduled Halt* and *Skylight*) with Smith/Doorstop and also a full collection *A Guided Tour of the Ice House* (2011)

Elizabeth Burns has published four collections, most recently *Held* (Polygon, 2010), and won the 2009 Michael Marks Award for Poetry Pamphlets. She lives in Lancaster, and teaches creative writing.

Marianne Burton's pamphlet *The Devil's Cut* was a Poetry Book Society choice. Her collection *She Inserts the Key* was published by Seren in April 2013.

Maggie Butt's four collections of poetry include two which are illustrated: *Sancti Clandestini: Undercover Saints* and *Ally Pally Prison Camp*; one of short poems: *petite* and her first collection *Lipstick*.

Caroline Carver lived in Bermuda, Jamaica and Canada before returning to the UK to live by the sea in Cornwall. She's a National Poetry prize winner and has published four collections.

A C Clarke's latest collections are *A Natural Curiosity* (New Voices Press 2012), shortlisted for the 2012 Callum Macdonald Memorial Award and *Fr Meslier's Confession* (Oversteps Books, 2012).

Anne Cluysenaar's most recent collection *Migrations* appeared from Cinnamon Press in autumn 2011. Her poem-diary *From Seen to Unseen and Back* is due from the same publisher in 2014.

Rose Cook has been published by HappenStance *Everyday Festival* (2009) and by Oversteps Books *Taking Flight* (2009). Her new collection *Notes From a Bright Field* will be out this year.

Pamela Coren taught English at the University of Leicester, has published a fair bit, including a collection, *The Blackbird Inspector* (Laurel Books). She lives in Cumbria, neighboured by Rough Fell sheep and curlews.

Doris Corti, born in London, has now retired to Yorkshire. She has one collection (Headland), is widely published in magazines and anthologies and is Poetry Columnist for *Writing Magazine*. She leads poetry classes for the University of the Third Age.

Kathryn Daszkiewicz was born in the north east and now lives and works in Lincolnshire. Her collections *In the Dangerous Cloakroom* and *Taking Flight* are published by Shoestring Press.

Ann Drysdale has published five poetry collections, as well as memoir, essays and a gonzo guidebook to the City of Newport. She lives in a mining town in South Wales.

Fiona Durance's writing has featured in numerous magazines and anthologies, in theatres, galleries and on radio. She loves the vastness of the open sea and the microcosms of rock pools.

Hilary Elfick's extensive travel is reflected in her ten collections. In her seventies she still spends time in small boats, and is a birding guide in New Zealand for several months a year.

Sylvia Fairley has lived and worked in East Anglia for many years as a professional flautist and teacher. She now divides her time between music and writing poetry.

Sally Festing's second chapbook is *Salaams* (Happenstance, 2009). She runs Saltmarsh Poetry in North Norfolk's Burnhams, and her sixth prose volume, *Showmen: the Voice of Travelling Fair People*, is out this year.

Kate Foley, former midwife and archaeological conservator lives between Amsterdam and Suffolk where she writes, reviews, helps edit Versal magazine, leads workshops. Just out, her fifth collection *One Window North*.

Angela France's publications include *Occupation* (Ragged Raven Press 2009), *Lessons in Mallemaroking* (Nine Arches Press 2011); and *Hide* (Nine Arches Press, 2013). Angela is features editor of *Iota* and she runs a reading series, 'Buzzwords'.

Wendy French has two full collections of poetry published. She won the Hippocrates Poetry and Medicine prize for the NHS section in 2010 and was awarded second prize in 2011.

Anne-Marie Fyfe's latest collection is *Understudies:* (Seren Books, 2010); she has run *Coffee-House Poetry*'s readings at London's *Troubadour* since 1997, and was chair of the *Poetry Society* from 2006-2009.

Katherine Gallagher is a widely-published London poet. She has five full collections, most recently *Carnival Edge: New & Selected Poems* (Arc, 2010). She represented Australia as a Parnassus Poet in 2012.

Geraldine Green has read widely in the UK, USA, Italy and Greece. *The Other Side of the Bridge* was published July 2012. *Salt Road* will be published summer 2013.

Gabriel Griffin is founder/organizer *Poetry on the Lake* events, Lake Orta, Italy and edits annual anthologies. Prized in competitions, published *Temenos, Scintilla, Peterloo,* et al. Collections: *Campango and the Mouthbrooders, Transumanza*.

Vona Groarke was born in Ireland and now lives in the UK. She teaches in the Centre for New Writing, University of Manchester. *Spindrift*, a PBS Recommendation for Autumn 2009, is her fifth collection from Gallery Press.

June Hall has published two collections, *The Now of Snow* (2004) and *Bowing to Winter* (2010). She's now working on a third, plus an anthology with R V Bailey of contemporary poetry of loss.

Susanna Harding is a writer and theatre practitioner. Her poems have been published in *The New Writer, The Interpreter's House, Equinox, Orbis* and *Smiths Knoll*. She lives in the Staffordshire Moorlands.

Jo Haslam lives and writes in Yorkshire. In the past three years she has won the Mslexia competition, 2nd prize in the National and the Straid award for a full collection *On the Kiso Road* (Templar).

Joy Howard has edited six anthologies and had two collections of her own poetry published since her retirement from 'proper' work in 2005. She lives in West Yorkshire.

Lesley Ingram was born in Yorkshire, lives in Ledbury. She has a Masters in Creative Writing and is working towards a first collection based on the artworks of Maggie Taylor.

Maria Jastrzębska's third collection is *At The Library of Memories* (Waterloo Press, 2013). She co-translated *Elsewhere* by Iztok Osojnik (Pighog Press, 2011). Her drama *Dementia Diaries* toured nationally in 2011.

Bernie Kenny lives in Dalkey, Co. Dublin, has published five poetry collections with Boland Press and *Gone to Earth*, translations from Irish (Black Mountain Press).

Angela Kirby, Lancashire born, now lives in London. Author of five non fiction books, her poems are translated into Rumanian. Her third collection, *A Scent of Winter*, has recently been published by Shoestring Press.

Wendy Klein is published in many magazines and anthologies. Her first collection from Cinnamon Press was *Cuba in the Blood*, and her second, *Anything in Turquoise*, also from Cinnamon is just out.

Stevie Krayer's publications include two collections of poetry and a translation of R M Rilke's *The Book of Hours*. She is currently co-editing an anthology of poetry by Quakers with R V Bailey.

Thelma Laycock, poet and retreat leader, lives in Leeds . She was a long-term editor and reviewer for *Gabriel* magazine. She has three pamphlets published and one full collection, *A Persistence of Colour*.

Gill Learner has been published widely, including in previous Grey Hen anthologies, and has won awards. Her first collection, *The Agister's Experiment* (Two Rivers Press, 2011) has been generously reviewed.

Eleanor Livingstone's *Even the Sea* (Red Squirrel Press, 2010) was shortlisted for the London New Poetry award for first collections. She is Director of the StAnza festival.

Janet Loverseed has poems in many magazines and anthologies and she has twice been a prizewinner in the Grey Hen competition. Her pamphlet *The Under-Ripe Banana* is published by HappenStance.

Rosemary McLeish is 67 and lives in Kent. She started writing poetry at the age of 40. She is an artist and shows her poetry in exhibitions.

Char March is an award-winning writer with five poetry collections, six BBC radio plays, and seven stage plays. Her short story collection '*Something Vital Fell Through*' is published summer 2013.

Alwyn Marriage is widely published in magazines and anthologies and reads at literary festivals in Britain and abroad. The latest of Alwyn's seven books, *festo*, was published in 2012.

Gerda Mayer, born in Czechoslovakia, came to England aged eleven. She has many collections from a variety of publishers. Her *Monkey on the Analysts Couch* was a Poetry Book Society recommendation.

Paula Meehan was born in Dublin where she still lives to the north of the city beside the sea. Her latest collection from Carcanet is *Painting Rain*.

Lyn Moir has published four collections, two with Arrowhead Press and two with Calder Wood Press. She lives in St. Andrews. She is working on a fifth collection.

Jenny Morris is an award-winning writer whose poems have appeared in many magazines, anthologies and in three collections, including *Lunatic Moon*. She lives in Norfolk.

Ruth O'Callaghan is a Hawthornden Fellow, tutor, mentor, reviewer, interviewer and adjudicator. Translated into six languages, she reads extensively in Asia, Europe, USA (gold medal in Taiwan). *The Silence Unheard* (Shoestring) is her fourth collection

Meg Peacocke says she has lived too many lives to want to list them now, but she hopes her poems will speak for some of them.

Jo Peters won the Lostock Poetry Prize and was second in the Torbay Poetry Competition in 2012. Now living in Yorkshire, she has fond childhood memories of the Devonshire coast.

Katrina Porteous lives by the sea in Northumberland. Best known for radio poems like *Dunstanburgh*, she also writes fishing history. Her publications include *The Lost Music* and *The Blue Lonnen*.

Joan Poulson is a poet, dramatist and children's writer. Her poetry is published in 300+ anthologies for all ages, her own books are in 660+ libraries internationally.

Caroline Price is a violinist and teacher living in Kent. Her most recent poetry collection is *Wishbone* (Shoestring Press, 2008). She is currently working on a novel.

Judith Priestman is a manuscript curator who lives and works in Oxfordshire, about as far removed from the sea as it is possible to be.

Maggie Rabatski comes from the isle of Harris but lives in Glasgow. She writes in both Gaelic and English. Her second poetry pamphlet *Holding* was recently published by New Voices Press.

Elisabeth Rowe writes serious poetry and comic/satirical verse. Her three collections are 'Surface Tension' (Peterloo Poets), 'Thin Ice' and 'Taking Shape' (Oversteps Books). She has always been in love with the sea.

Hermione Sandall spent her childhood by the Solent. She and her husband sailed to the West Indies in 1971/2, returned to teaching, and sailed in European waters during their holidays.

Carole Satyamurti is a poet and sociologist. She has published six collections of poetry, and is currently completing a verse abridgement of the Indian epic, the *Mahabharata*.

Myra Schneider's recent collections are *Circling The Core* (Enitharmon, 2008) and *What Women Want* (Second Light Publications, 2012). Other publications include books about personal writing. She is consultant to the Second Light Network.

Gina Shaw is a regular contributor to Grey Hen anthologies. She likes walking by the sea but will settle for a bus-ride past that bit of the River Wharfe she claims is hers.

Penelope Shuttle lives in Cornwall, and is current Chair of Falmouth Poetry Group. Her most recent publication is *Unsent: Selected and New Poems 1980–2012*, (Bloodaxe Books, 2012).

Pat Simmons worked in charity communications, and started writing poetry when she retired. She has had poems published in several anthologies, and was winner of the 2010 Grey Hen Press national poetry competition.

Pauline Stainer has published eight collections with Bloodaxe, the latest being *Tiger Facing the Mist*. She is a Hawthornden Fellow and was awarded a Cholmondeley award by the Society of Authors

Anne Stewart (MADist) studied at Sheffield Hallam University with Sean O'Brien. She won the Bridport Prize in 2008. Her collection *The Janus Hour* was published by Oversteps Books in 2010.

Sheila Templeton is an award winning poet currently living in Glasgow, with two poetry collections, *Slow Road Home* published by Makar Press 2004 and *Digging For Light* published by New Voices Press 2011.

Fiona Ritchie Walker is a Scot, now living in North East England. Her latest poetry collection, *The Second Week of the Soap*, is published by Red Squirrel Press.

Jean Watkins's poems have been published in *Mslexia, Magma, South* and many anthologies. Her first collection *Scrimshaw* is forthcoming from Two Rivers Press in June 2013.

Christine Webb has published two full collections, *After Babel* (Peterloo Poets, 2004) and *Catching Your Breath* (Cinnamon Press, 2011) as well as appearing in a number of periodicals and anthologies.

Lynne Wycherley is a poet of wild places, birds, and shifting light. She often draws inspiration from the sea-lit margins of Britain. Her *Luminous: New & Selected Poems* is forthcoming from Shoestring Press

Acknowledgements

ANN ALEXANDER 'Rain Coming' *Too Close* (Ward Wood, 2010); 'The Sea at Night' *Facing Demons* (Peterloo Poets, 2002); 'On Land, He Is a Chapel Man' *Nasty, British & Short* (Peterloo Poets, 2007). JEAN ATKIN 'Lost at Sea' 'Becoming Variable' 'Shoal' 'Janet Hunter Remembers her Man' and 'The Ditty Box of Thomas Gilbert Hunter Aiken' *Lost at Sea* (Roncadora Press, 2011) and *Not Lost Since Last Time* (Oversteps, 2013). R V BAILEY 'Whitley Bay' *Marking Time* (Peterloo, 2004). PAT BORTHWICK 'Kleptomaniac' *Between Clouds and Caves* (Littlewood Arc 1988) and *Swim* (Mudfrog Press, 2005). ALISON BRACKENBURY 'On the Sailing Boat' published in *Stand.* CAROLE BROMLEY 'Telescope' *Unscheduled Halt* (Smith/Doorstop, 2005); 'Desirable Residence' published in *South.* ELIZABETH BURNS 'Making a Landscape' and 'Painting the Sea' *The Lantern Bearers* (Shoestring, 2007). MARIANNE BURTON '7am: Mauritius: To the Sea' *She Inserts the Key* (Seren, 2013). MAGGIE BUTT 'My Second Life' *petite* (Hearing Eye, 2010); 'Fish Wife' *Lipstick* (Greenwich Exchange, 2007). A C CLARKE Rubh an Eun published in *Fras.* ANNE CLUYSENAAR 'Hearing Your Words' published in *ARTEMISpoetry.* ROSE COOK 'The Way Freedoms Are Dreamt' *Taking Flight* (HappenStance, 2009); 'The Storm' published in *Anemone Sidecar.* DORIS CORTI 'Slapton Sands' *The Tumbling Sky* (Headland, 1998). HILARY ELFICK 'Baptism' *The Horse Might Sing* (Envoi, 1990). ANN DRYSDALE 'Old Boats' *Discussing Wittgenstein* and *Quaintness and Other Offences* (both Cinnamon Press, 2009). SALLY FESTING 'Sea Wall, Overy Staithe' An earlier version of this poem appeared in *Between the Land and the Sea* (Tim Fisher and Kevin Crossley-Holland eds. Community Publication, 2012). KATE FOLEY 'Soft Engineering' and 'Sometimes I Long for Dry Land' *Soft Engineering* (Onlywomen Press, 1994). ANGELA FRANCE 'Intertidal' published in the ezine *Qarrtsiluni*; 'Sea Hare' *Occupation* (Ragged Raven Press, 2009), previously published in *Iota.* ANNE-MARIE FYFE 'Take to the Sea', 'To the Lamp Room' and '6, Sloop Lane' *Understudies* (Seren, 2010). KATHERINE GALLAGHER 'The Lifeboat Shed' and 'Grey Forms – (1922)' *Carnival-Edge* (Arc Publications, 2006). GERALDINE GREEN 'Well Drilled' *Salt Road* (Indigo Dreams, 2013); previously published in *Poetry Cornwall.* GABRIEL GRIFFIN 'Lament for an Illegal Immigrant' published in *Barnet Arts Anthology* (2005). VONA GROARKE 'The Idea of the Atlantic' *Shale* (The Gallery Press, 1994); 'Pier' *Spindrift* (The Gallery Press, 2009). JUNE HALL 'Charting the Tides' published in *Acumen.* SUSANNA HARDING 'Ghost Ship' published in *Orbis*; 'Floating' published in *Equinox.* BERNIE KENNY 'Sceilig Michíl' *Alawys Dalkey Always the Sea* (Boland Press, 2011). ANGELA KIRBY 'Julia's Doves' *Dirty Work* (Shoestring Press, 2008), also published in *Magma*; 'Leviathan' published in *Moonstone.* WENDY KLEIN 'Sea Facing' *Cuba in the Blood* (Cinnamon Press, 2009). GILL LEARNER 'Resurrection' published in *ARTEMISpoetry.* ELEANOR LIVINGSTONE 'With Salt' (different version) *Even the Sea* (Red Squirrel Press, 2010). GERDA MAYER 'Seafarer' first published in *Ambit*, now in

Prague Winter (Hearing Eye, 2005). PAULA MEEHAN 'Ashes' *Painting Rain* (Carcanet, 2000). LYN MOIR 'Survey Ship' *Easterly, Force 10* (Calder Wood Press, 2009), and 'St. Andrews Harbour' *Breakers' Yard* (Arrowhead Press, 2003). RUTH O'CALLAGHAN 'Shore to Ship' *Where Acid Has Etched* (bluechrome, 2007). M R PEACOCKE 'Going West' *Speaking of the Dead* (Peterloo, 2003). KATRINA PORTEOUS 'Cathy' and 'Alnmouth' *The Blue Lonnen* (Jardine, 2007). 'The Sea Inside' *The Lost Music* (Bloodaxe, 1996). 'Hermit Crab' an extract from *The Refuge Box*, first broadcast on 'Between the Ears' (BBC Radio 3, 2007). CAROLINE PRICE 'Current' published in *Cyphers*. MAGGIE RABATSKI 'At Borve Cemetery, 2010' published in *Northwords Now and Holding* (New Voices Press, 2012). HERMIONE SANDALL 'The Evening Swim'published in *Poetry, Therapy and the Emotional Life* (Radcliffe Publishing, 2005). CAROLE SATYAMURTI 'Day Trip' and 'Chesil Beach' *Stitching the Dark: New and Selected Poems* (Bloodaxe, 2005); 'The Day I knew I wouldn't live forever' *Countdown* (Bloodaxe, 2011). MYRA SCHNEIDER 'Blakeney' *Circling The Core* (Enitharmon Press, 2008). PAULINE STAINER 'Turner is lashed to the mast' *The Ice-Pilot Speaks* (Bloodaxe, 1994); 'The Seals' and 'Beyond the garden Gilgamesh saw the sea' *Parable Island* (Bloodaxe, 1999); 'The Ship's Gardener' *Crossing the Snowline* (Bloodaxe, 2008). SHEILA TEMPLETON. 'Eavesdropping' *Tracks in the Sand* and 'Lighthouses' *Shorelines* (New Voices Press anthologies, 2011 and 2012). FIONA RITCHIE WALKER 'Estuary Island' *Garibaldi's Legs* (Iron Press, 2005). 'The Price of Gutted Herring' *Angus Palette* (Sand, 2006), *New Writing11* (British Council/Picador, 2002). LYNNE WYCHERLEY 'The Last Lighthouse' Acknowledgment: The Last Lighthouse *North Flight* (Shoestring Press, 2006)

Joy Howard is the founder of Grey Hen Press, which specialises in publishing the work of older women poets. Her poems have featured in several anthologies: *Beautiful Barbarians* (Onlywomen, 1987), *Dancing the Tightrope* (Women's Press, 1987), *Naming the Waves* (Virago, 1988), *Not for the Academy* (Onlywomen, 1999), *The Argent Moon* (Pembrokeshire Press, 2007), and *The Listening Shell* (Headland Press, 2010). She has edited five previous Grey Hen Press anthologies, and published a collection of her own poems *Exit Moonshine* (Grey Hen, 2009) about her 'coming out' experiences in the 1980s. She has been published in *Sofia*, *Sphinx*, ARTEMIS*poetry*, *Lavender Review*, *The Interpreter's House*, *The Frogmore Papers* and *Orbis*. Her poems can be found online at *Guardian Unlimited* and *poetry p f*, and feature in *'Poems While You Wait'* at St James's Hospital in Leeds. Her latest collection, *Refurbishment*, was published by Ward Wood in 2011.

www.greyhenpress.com